Neither Foe nor Friend

The American Image of Russia in Transition

von

Katrin Ullmann

Tectum Verlag
Marburg 2005

Ullmann, Katrin:
Neither Foe nor Friend.
The American Image of Russia in Transition.
/ von Katrin Ullmann
- Marburg : Tectum Verlag, 2005
ISBN 978-3-8288-8785-5

© Tectum Verlag

Tectum Verlag
Marburg 2005

Table of Contents

1. Introduction

This work is an attempt to find an answer to the question of how the Americans' perception of, and relationship to, Russia have changed since the former adversary "opened its doors" to the West. For several decades, the Iron Curtain had separated the two peoples on both sides of the Atlantic Ocean by barriers of misunderstanding, suspicion and alienation. The accession of Mikhail Gorbachev to power in the mid-1980s suddenly opened one of the most remarkable chapters in America's relationship with the Soviet Union. Americans and Russians, in the course of the following two decades would interact to an extent never anticipated and come to call each other partners, or even friends. The word friendship, however, is often used superficially. The appropriateness of its usage with regard to American-Russian relations needs to be analyzed seriously and critically.

In the winter of 1985-1986, a research project called "Friends and Enemies," asked 57 introductory psychology students what it means to call another country an "enemy" or a "friend" of the United States.[1] Inherently, the results of this study are not representative of all Americans. Still, the definitions these students gave can serve as a basis and guideline for finding answers about how, from the American point of view, the image of Russia has since changed. The most frequently given definitions and criteria for an "enemy of the United States" were as follows (Note: The respondents were allowed to give more than one answer):

It has different values, ideals, systems. (60%)
- disagrees with our politics, values, beliefs
- has a different non-democratic government/system
- is communist

It is a threat or danger. (55%)
- is a threat, danger (not specified)
- is prepared to fight, has nuclear weapons
- sides against us in any conflict, plots against us

It is unfriendly, hostile, anti-U.S. (30%)
- spreads propaganda against us
- there is hatred/tensions on both sides

---

[1] For coverage of the entire project, which was conducted at the Department of Psychology at New York University, see Holt, Robert R.: College Students' Definitions and Images of Enemies, in: *Journal of Social Issues*, Vol. 45, No 2, 1989, pp. 33-50.

It is uncooperative, competitive, uncommunicative (21%)
- bad communication
- wants to hurt us economically, have trade war with us
- wants to be more powerful than us, competes

In the same project, the respondents were asked to indicate, for a list of nations, whether each of them was friend, enemy or neither. The percentage citing the USSR as enemy was 87 percent. At the time of the project, the mean age of the respondents was 19. While we know that when they were young students a large majority of them perceived the Soviet Union as an enemy, there is no information on what these, now middle-aged, adults think of Russia today. One could at least speculate by analyzing whether Russia today matches the given definitions of a "friend of the United States," which were as follows:

It is an ally, helps us/we help them. (47%)
- we rely on each other
- it supports our interests
- it will not oppose us militarily

We have similar values, policies, goals. (41%)
- is a free/democratic country, not communist
- is procapitalist, anticommunist
- takes our advice, complies with our wishes

We trade with them, have cultural exchange, good communications. (25%)

It is peaceful, no threat, does not hurt/infringe on our citizens. (12%)
- can travel there safely
- no antagonism

These general definitions form starting points for my explorative journeys from the period of renewed Cold War tensions in the early 1980s, through Gorbachev's years and into current times; searching for patterns of change in the Americans' relationship to Russia. The main idea is to make a comparison of the current status quo with the situation prior to Gorbachev's accession to power. Although Americans and Russians no longer appose each other as enemies, they remain separated by history, distance, culture, language and misunderstandings. Russia finds itself in a pending situation. From the American point of view, it is neither a foe, nor a friend. It is, instead, a more or less cooperative partner, which in some aspects does not agree with American views, but has a fair chance of becoming a serious ally and friend in the future.

In structuring the thesis, I devoted one chapter to the rapprochement of both nations on a government-to-government level, another to the American public's perception of Russia, and a third to the extent Americans have familiarized with the Russian culture and the Russian people. Many respondents of the "Friends and Enemies" project defined a friend of the United States as a country that both helps the U.S. and receives help from the U.S. In a broader sense, they imagined a country that "supports our interests." Moreover, many of them perceived a national friend as a nation, which has values, policies, and goals similar to those of the United States, mainly referring to democracy and capitalism as the basic rules of the society. With this in mind, the first part of the first chapter covers how and to what extent the two countries have approached and cooperated with each other on a government-to-government level since the mid-1980s. At the same time, it serves as a historical background against which the following parts of the thesis should be viewed. The events in the governmental arena are, for the most part, what Americans see, hear and read about in the media. Hence, they have a tremendous effect on how Americans perceive their relationship with the Russians. The agreements signed on the presidential level constitute the foundation for the development of large-scale American-Russian contacts on a people-to-people basis.

The main reason for cooperation on the government-to-government level was a specific kind of reciprocal dependency. Moscow depended on Washington for financial backing and political support, while American leaders depended on Russian leaders and their governments to keep Russia stable and peaceful. The United States did not want Russia to again become a threat, but a trustworthy partner who would comply with U.S. wishes. Against this background, the second part of the first chapter discusses the scope of U.S. direct financial aid to Russia and the depth of Russia's compliance with Americans' expectations regarding the establishment of a strong democracy and a free market economy, as well as the maintenance of a pro-American stance. In this part of the thesis, I deliberately quote numerous American Russia observers to show a judgment of Russia's transition from the American point of view.

In the second chapter, I demonstrate trends in American attitudes toward the USSR, and later Russia, from the beginning of the 1980s until today. These findings are based on a careful analysis of American opinion polls. Several tendencies have crystallized in the public opinion with regard to the former Cold War enemy. First of all, the perception of the Soviet Union as a threat declined sharply throughout the late 1980s. I found three major trends in the general attitudes toward the Soviet Union and later Russia. First, a declining hostility combined with a rising favorability toward the Soviet Union throughout the second half of the 1980s. Second, a cooling trend in the favorability toward Russia throughout the 1990s, which is in accordance with the cooling period in American-Russian relations on a government-to-government level at the same period of time. Finally, a warming trend in recent years, especially since the moment after the terrorist attacks of September 11, 2001, when Russia expressed solidarity with the U.S. in the fight against terrorism. Although today a majority of Americans again have a favorable opinion of Russia, this figure remains far below the one of 1993, when the percentage of Americans having a positive perception of Russia peaked. The current perception of Russia is rather ambivalent. While for most Americans, Russia seems to be a friendly nation, the American public has not yet completely discounted the idea of Russia becoming a threat again in the future. Although Russia is currently viewed as a partner, it is not yet an ally. The fact that a large majority of Americans today wish to see Russia join NATO, however, shows that they want Russia to become a serious ally in the near future.

The last and most extensive chapter focuses on the American approach to the Russians and their culture. In the first part of the chapter, I put an emphasis on the barriers to cross-cultural communication and understanding between Americans and Russians. I stress that it is important to draw a distinction between having stereotypes on the one hand, and knowing about the real differences between the two cultures on the other. In the second part, I evaluate how much Americans have learned about their former enemy to be able to overcome these barriers. I analyze the quantitative USSR/Russia coverage on the major American TV news channels and in the *New York Times*. Moreover, I examine the history of Soviet- and post-Soviet studies and Russian language study in the United States. The most obvious tendency I found in all of these aspects was an alarming decline in Americans' interest in Russia and the Russian culture throughout the last decade.

The final part of the third chapter concentrates on the extent of direct contact Americans have experienced with Russians and their country in the course of the last two decades. Throughout the Cold War years, cultural contacts between Americans and Russians, though very limited, had already seemed to be the sole possibility to humanize the relationship and to soften the mutual demonic image. The end of the Cold War has broadened the nature and the scope of the American-Russian cultural relationship dramatically. This study defines cultural relations in broad terms, including activities normally considered "cultural" in nature – literature, art, music, etc. – as well as cooperative activities in the fields of science, technology, business, tourism and other areas in which Americans and Russians associate as human beings.

I COOPERATION AND COMMON VALUES

The era in which the United States and Russia saw each other as an enemy or strategic threat has ended. We are partners and we will cooperate to advance stability, security, and economic integration, and to jointly counter global challenges and to help resolve regional conflicts.

-- Joint Declaration on New U.S.-Russia Relationship (2002)[2]

2. From Competition to Cooperation

Cold War Warriors

For more than forty years, the Soviet Union and the United States, the only two world powers left after World War II, had been the main global competitors of the Cold War. Both nations struggled for global domination by building and enlarging spheres of influence and attracting allies. They competed not only ideologically; but militarily, economically, scientifically and even culturally. The guidelines of American diplomacy throughout the Cold War era, as Stanley Hoffmann observed, had been containment and coexistence: "containment in order to limit the expansion of Soviet power and influence, coexistence because – even before nuclear parity – most Americans have wanted to prevent the superpowers' rivalry from leading to the catastrophe of nuclear war."[3]

After détente, a period of rapprochement between the two adversaries in the 1970s, the tensions rose again in the early 1980s. It was the time of President Ronald Reagan's raw anticommunist rhetoric and actions. The Reagan Administration discouraged arms-control talks, stepped up aid to anticommunist movements, announced the Strategic Defense Initiative (SDI, also known as "Star Wars") and introduced the largest peacetime military budget in history. While Reagan turned to military solutions, in the Soviet Union, a new younger and reform-minded generation of Soviet officials came to power in 1985 under the leadership of General Secretary of the Communist Party, Mikhail Gorbachev.

---

[2] The White House Office of Press Secretary: "Joint Declaration on New US-Russia Relationship," Date: 20020524; Internet Site: <http://www.whitehouse.gov/news/releases/2001/11/20011113-4. html> (accessed 25 November 2003).

[3] Stanley Hoffmann, The United States and the Soviet Union, in: *Western Approaches to the Soviet Union*, Michael Mandelbaum (ed.), New York, Council on Foreign Relations Books, 1988, pp. 79-111.

The Reagan-Gorbachev Rapprochement

Because of the rising peace movement in Europe, the antinuclear movement in the U.S.,[4] and the general decline in public support (due to the Iran-Contra scandal[5] and a huge deficit in the U.S. budget), Reagan began to apply a more communicative approach toward the Soviet Union in the mid 1980s. In November 1985, the first U.S.-Soviet summit in six years was held in Geneva. This was a revolutionary event in and of itself. Despite the lack of substance, the summit meeting had a profound impact on symbolical terms. Both sides agreed that a nuclear war cannot be won and must never be fought. Television pictures showing Reagan and Gorbachev smiling together were a visible sign of the restored dialogue between the two main adversaries of the Cold War. No serious agreements had been reached on key issues like arms control and regional issues, such as Afghanistan, Angola or Nicaragua. Both nations tried to influence the political course in these regions with regard to their own, mostly ideological, strategic and economical interests.[6]

In terms of renewed people-to-people contacts, however, the summit turned out to be very successful. Secretary of state, George Shultz, and foreign minister, Eduard Shevardnadze, signed the Agreement on Contacts and Exchanges in Scientific, Educational and Cultural Fields, which served as a basis for large-scale exchange initiatives and contained measures to promote Russian language studies in the United States and English language studies in the USSR.[7] Moreover, the Civil Aviation Agreement was initialed soon after the summit with the purpose of restoring Pan American and Aeroflot direct lines between the two countries. After Geneva, both leaders met once a year for a total of four summit meetings until the end of Reagan's second term in January 1989. Despite Gorbachev making breathtaking proposals on arms reduction, a proposal for eliminating all nuclear weapons included, Reagan insisted on SDI. This intention not only violated the ABM treaty,[8] it also jeopardized the prospects of a real breakthrough with regard to arms reduction since the Soviet

---

[4] For a detailed historical analysis of the American Nuclear Freeze movement and the influence it had on U.S. foreign policy, see: David Cortright, *Peace Works – The Citizen's Role in Ending the Cold War*, Boulder, San Francisco, Oxford, Westview Press, 1993.

[5] The Iran-Contra affair was a national crisis that erupted in 1986. Reagan had ordered the National Security Council (NSC) to carry out a covert project to trade arms to Iran in return for the release of U.S. hostages held in Lebanon. Because he also empowered the NSC secretly to aid Nicaraguan *contras*, the two operations eventually commingled, when profits from the Iranian arms sales had been diverted to the *contras*.

[6] Thomas G. Paterson, J. Garry Clifford, Hagan, Kenneth J.: *American Foreign Relations, Volume 2 – A History Since 1895*, Boston, New York, Houston Mifflin Company, 2000, pp. 430-440.

[7] Joint Soviet-United States Statement on the Summit Meeting in Geneva, November 21, 1985; Internet site: <http://www.reagan.utexas.edu/resources/speeches/1985/112185.ahtm> (accessed 22 December 2003).

[8] ABM = Anti-ballistic missile system; The ABM treaty was signed in 1972 and limited the deployment of ABMs for each nation to two sites.

side considered this topic to be a crucial factor for reaching any kind of common ground.

Only because of the good relationship between Shultz and Shevardnadze, the INF treaty[9] was signed in December 1987 at the Washington Summit. Each side would destroy all of its heavy land-based missiles armed with multiple warheads within the next three years. This was, in a way, a real breakthrough. It meant that an entire class of U.S. and Soviet nuclear arms would be completely eliminated. Although this agreement covered only five percent of the entire nuclear arsenal of both nations, it had considerable psychological, political and military strategic significance.[10] Michael Mandelbaum pointed out that these were "the weapons that the U.S. considers most threatening because they are most useful for a preemptive attack."[11]

Another important agreement was signed even before the meeting in Washington. It was an accord on resuming cooperation in peaceful exploration of space, which had been in effect from 1972 to 1982, but as a sanction against Soviet pressure on Poland was not renewed.[12] The Washington summit was the first in the capital since fourteen years. It gave Gorbachev the chance to spread his charm throughout the United States. The so-called "Gorbymania" had affected American public opinion. Shortly after the last summit meeting between Reagan and Gorbachev in Moscow (1988), a Harris poll showed a phenomenal 77 percent of Americans polled rated Gorbachev's performance as the leader of the Soviet Union as either "pretty good" (52%) or even "excellent" (25%).[13]

Throughout the Reagan presidency, little progress was made in terms of economic relations with the Soviet Union. Trade remained low and the U.S. government made no move to normalize trade relations, neither with regard to credits nor the Jackson-Vanik amendment, which barred "most favored nation" (MFN) status to the Soviet Union until emigration restrictions on Soviet Jews were erased.[14] Reagan's stubborn insistence on SDI, ongoing discrepancies over regional issues, the lack of trade relations, as well as various spy incidents made it difficult to achieve more trust on both sides throughout Reagan's second term.

---

[9] INF = Intermediate-Range Nuclear Forces

[10] Raymond L. Garthoff, *The Great Transition: American-Soviet relations and the end of the Cold War*, Washington, D.C., The Brookings Institution, pp. 326-327.

[11] Michael Mandelbaum, Ending the Co d War, in: *Foreign Affairs* 68/2, 1989, pp. 26-27.

[12] Garthoff, cited above, p. 312.

[13] Source: Harris (Louis Harris and Associates), Date: 07/1988; Internet site: <http://www.irss.unc. edu/data_archive/pollsearch.html> (accessed 14 November 2003).

[14] MFN is used to denote nondiscriminatory treatment of a trading partner; MFN has been used in international agreements and in U.S. law to denote the fundamental trade principle of nondiscriminatory treatment of a trading partner. MFN has been renewed annually under a waiver of the Jackson-Vanik amendment to the 1974 Trade Act.

Concerns about Soviet espionage, during the first half of 1987, even tended to dominate the relationship in the eyes of the American public.[15]

While Gorbachev's reforms "*glasnost*'" and "*perestroika*" were watched with satisfaction by Americans, it was clear that he would hold on to communism as the basis of the Soviet system. Through the withdrawal of Soviet troops from Afghanistan in 1988/99, however, he signaled to Americans the seriousness of his efforts to change Soviet foreign policy. Graham T. Allison, in 1988, concluded: "Gorbachev has accepted defeat, with only the fig leaf of calling it stalemate and without even demanding a decent interval. This realism is the strongest evidence so far that he may genuinely believe some of the more unlikely things he says."[16] The historian Peter G. Boyle noted that as Reagan left office, the U.S.' relationship with the Soviet Union "had been transformed out of all recognition" from the beginning of the 1980s.[17]

Caution

When in the countries of Eastern Europe by the end of 1989 the communist governments had collapsed, the newly elected president George Bush had almost no time to absorb the implications of these rapid developments. His response to the collapse of Communism was "caution". Bush met with Gorbachev only once a year. Although the START I[18] treaty was signed at the third summit in August 1991 and SDI (because of waning public support) led to reduction in funding, the Bush administration had not made any significant progress on arms reduction.[19] American trade with the Soviet Union remained meek. Gorbachev had to deal with more and more problems at home, but the Bush administration did not come up with economic assistance.[20] While economic relations and arms reduction talks were characterized by slow progress, U.S.-Soviet relations during the Bush-Gorbachev period were marked by a flood of exchange agreements. At the three summit meetings, numerous routine agreements had been reached with regard to educational, cultural, scientific and interpersonal exchanges. For example, the 1000/1000 University Undergraduate Exchange program was announced at the Malta Summit in December 1989,[21] while in the next year the two sides agreed upon the

---

[15] Garthoff, cited above, p. 311.

[16] Graham T. Allison, Testing Gorbachev, in: *Foreign Affairs* 67/1, 1988, p. 27.

[17] Peter G. Boyle, *American-Soviet Relations – From the Russian Revolution to the fall of Communism*, London, New York, Routledge, 1993, p. 224.

[18] START = Strategic Arms Reduction Treaty.

[19] Garthoff, cited above, p. 466.

[20] Boyle, cited above, p. 239.

[21] USIA fact sheet, "USIA Programs and Initiatives in NIS," Date: 19930402; Public Diplomacy Query (PDQ) database of the U.S. Department of State; Internet site: <http://pdq.state.gov>.

establishment of cultural centers and the expansion of civil aviation arrangements.[22]

Gorbachev, during his stay in Washington and Camp David in mid 1990, won the hearts of the American public a second time, deepening "Gorbymania" once more. The Soviet Union backed the United States in the effort to liberate Kuwait in early 1991. Graham Allison and Robert Blackwill, after the Golf War, pointed out:

> The day after Iraqi troops marched into Kuwait, both Baker and Shevardnadze jointly condemned the action and announced cutoff of arms to Iraq. In the weeks that followed the SU not only voted for each U.N. resolution condemning Iraq and demanding withdrawal, but also played an important role in persuading others to go along… Try to imagine the US-led international offensive against Saddam Hussein absent active Soviet cooperation.[23]

Despite a heavy recession during the winter of 1990/91, Gorbachev's reforms to introduce market economy in the Soviet Union got under way. Still, the Soviet leader insisted that his aim was to reform communism. He was increasingly dependent on conservative elements as he lost the support of public opinion and liberal reformers like Boris Yeltsin, who criticized the slow pace of his reforms.

In August 1991, the leaders of the conservative communist wing announced a take-over. The coup quickly collapsed because of massive demonstrations and armed forces refusing to obey orders. Yeltsin, who played a leading role during the demonstrations against the coup leaders, became the first democratically elected Russian President in June 1991. In August, Gorbachev resigned as head of the Communist Party. Four months later, he announced his resignation and the Soviet Union, on December 21, formally ceased to exist. The failed coup had a very significant implication. It doomed any prospect of a return to power of communist hardliners, marking the end of the Cold War and leaving the U.S. as the only surviving global superpower.

The "Honeymoon" Period

The years 1992 and 1993 in American-Russian relations often are referred to as the "honeymoon" period. The three Bush-Yeltsin summit meetings held in only thirteen months are the most visible sign for a much more active cooperation on the government-to-government level. One of the highest priorities of the Bush Administration was to ensure the integrity and security of the former Soviet

---

[22] Garthoff, cited above, p. 426.
[23] Graham Allison, Robert Blackwill, America's Stake in the Soviet Future, in: *Foreign Affairs* 70/3, 1991, p. 77.

nuclear arsenal through the Cooperative Threat Reduction (CTR) program, which was passed by Congress in December 1991 and is better known as the Nunn-Lugar program. It served as the basis for the transfer of American funds to assist Russia in dismantling weapons.[24] Arms reduction talks continued with the START II treaty signed in January 1993, which outlined provisions for the elimination of strategic arms to a third of the earlier stock.[25]

Another priority of the Bush Administration regarding U.S.-Russian relations was the promotion of democracy and a free market economy in Russia. The first milestone in the U.S.-Russian relationship within a new world order was the Camp David Declaration at the first summit in February 1992, when the two presidents agreed that their countries would not regard one another as "potential enemies".[26] In June, at the second summit in Washington the two leaders signed the Charter for American-Russian Partnership and Friendship. It contained a statement indicating that both countries are sharing common values and goals like international peace and security, democracy, economic freedom and the commitment of working together to meet these ends.[27] Finally, both sides ratified a bilateral trade agreement, and the United States granted MFN status to Russia, thereby paving the way for expanded economic relations.[28]

A few months after the Washington summit, in October 1992, the U.S. Congress passed the Freedom Support Act (FSA), an assistance package for Russia and the other new countries of the former Soviet Union. The initiative was designed to fund programs fostering the transition to a market economy and the democratization process in the Newly Independent States (NIS). It also considerably increased U.S.-NIS exchange programs, which meant a new focus on a people-to-people level. Russia, over the years would receive more than a third of the cumulative funds budgeted for these programs. The U.S Agency for International Development (USAID) administered most of the economy- and democracy-oriented assistance programs. The U.S. Department of Commerce

---

[24] "Nunn-Lugar Assistance to NIS Accelerated"—Third Pentagon Report regarding the progress of the Cooperative Threat Reduction program, Date: 19940829, PDQ database, Internet site: <http://pdq.state.gov> (accessed 26 November 2003). The Nunn-Lugar program is named after its legislative authors, Senator Sam Nunn (D-GA) and Richard Lugar (R-IN).

[25] For a detailed content analyses of the Start II treaty, see "Reducing the Threat of Weapons of Mass Destruction" – White House release, Date: 19960129, PDQ database; Internet site: <http://pdq.state.gov> (accessed 26 November 2003).

[26] "US-Russian Relations" – Excerpt from news conference, Camp David, Maryland, February 1, 1992, US Department of State Dispatch published by the Bureau of Public Affairs Vol.3, Number 5, Date: 19920203; PDQ database, Internet site: <http://pdq.state.gov> (accessed 25 October 2003).

[27] The White House Office of the Press Secretary: Fact Sheet on the Charter for American-Russian Partnership and Friendship, June 17, 1992; Internet site: <http://www.fas.org/spp/starwars/offdocs/b920617.htm> (accessed 15 October 2003).

[28] William H. Cooper, "Permanent Normal Trade Relations (PNTR) Status for Russia and U.S.-Russian Economic Ties", CRS Report for Congress, Order Code: RS21123, January 28, 2002.

supported business development while the U.S. Information Agency (USIA) (later renamed Bureau for Educational and Cultural Affairs) was mainly responsible for programs regarding U.S.-Russia people-to-people exchanges.

The newly elected Clinton Administration carried forward the bilateral and multilateral assistance programs begun by the Bush Administration. Clinton also continued and pressed the position taken by his predecessor on the issue of the ex-Soviet nuclear arsenal. The measures of the Nunn-Lugar program were greatly enlarged. In February 1993, one of the most notable agreements provided for the United States purchase of some 500 metric tons of highly enriched uranium over a 20-year period for approximately $12 billion. Russia, at its own facilities, would blend down its highly enriched uranium to provide the U.S. with low-enriched uranium, which could be directly used as nuclear fuel for U.S. reactors.[29] Clinton, as Bush before him, shared an interest in establishing a close and highly visible personal relationship with Yeltsin. Both would soon refer to each other as "my friend Bill" and "my friend Boris." Throughout the seven years of Clinton's presidency, both leaders met eighteen times. This in itself was a sign of growing normalcy in the relationship.

The first of their numerous summit meetings was held at Vancouver in April 1993, where talk about economic reform and democracy played as central a role as negotiations over nuclear weapons did in the past. The presidents agreed upon a new package of bilateral programs designed to address Russia's immediate human needs, contribute to the building of a market economy and increase cooperation in space and people-to-people exchanges. They agreed to establish a U.S.-Russian Commission on Technological Cooperation in the Fields of Energy and Space, later to be called the Gore-Chernomyrdin commission (named after Prime Minister Chernomyrdin and Vice President Gore, who headed the commission).[30] The new strategy toward Russia under President Clinton soon crystallized; the goal being a partnership with a democratic Russia and aid for President Yeltsin's government as the highest priority. Russia was to be assisted in the effort to transform its economy through a so-called "shock-therapy." To stimulate the American public's backing for financial aid to Russia, that support was to be projected in a deliberately optimistic fashion. In a statement before the Senate Foreign Relations Committee on April 20, 1993, Secretary of State Warren Christopher expressed this new strategy as follows:

---

[29] Nikhil Anand, Mary Byrd Davis, "USEC Privatization and the Russian HEU Agreement," Earth Island Institute, June 1999, updated November 2001, Internet site: <www.earthisland.org/yggdrasil/uep112_01. html> (accessed 23 October 2003).
[30] "Vancouver Declaration" – Joint Statement, Date: 19930404; PDQ database; Internet site: <http://pdq. state.gov> (accessed 26 November 2003).

President Clinton and I are convinced that this investment in Russia's democratic future is an essential investment in America's future. By making this investment, we can help turn our most dangerous enemy into an enduring partner. That, I believe, is a critical – indeed, a noble – mission.[31]

The Cooling Period

Some 97 agreements had been signed between 1992 and 1996 covering numerous aspects of cooperation.[32] At the Moscow Summit in January 1994, for example, both countries agreed that they would no longer target their nuclear missiles at each other. Thus, for the first time since the dawn of the nuclear age, they would not operate nuclear forces in a manner that presumes they are adversaries.[33] At the Washington Summit in September the same year, the presidents signed the Joint U.S.-Russian Statement on Trade, Economic Cooperation and Investment.[34] The establishment of a U.S. Foundation to Support Joint U.S.-NIS Research Efforts was agreed upon at the Moscow Summit held in May 1995. It was intended to support the expansion of cooperation between American and Russian scientists.[35] Guided by the provisions of the Charter for American-Russian Partnership and Friendship of 1992, the two governments signed the U.S.-Russia Memorandum of Understanding on the Principles of Cooperation in the Fields of Culture, the Humanities, the Social Sciences, Education and the Mass Media at the summit meeting held in Moscow in September 1998.[36]

Behind the scenes, however, U.S.-Russian relations in late 1993 had entered a "cooling period" that would last until the end of the decade. Although bilateral relations between the two countries had been very productive, frictions

---

[31] Statement by Secretary of State Warren Christopher before the Senate Foreign Relations Committee, Testimony on Assistance to Russia and Foreign Affairs Budget, Office of the Spokesman; U.S. Department of State, Washington D.C., April 20, 1993; Internet site: <http://dosfan.lib.uic.edu/ ERC/briefing/dossec/1993/9304/930420dossec.html>. (accessed 15 October 2003).

[32] Raymond L. Garthoff, The United States and the New Russia: The First Five Years, in: *Current History* 96/612, 1997, p. 307.

[33] US Department of State Dispatch: "The Moscow Declaration", Bureau of Public Affairs, Vol. 5, Supplement Number 1, January 1994, PDQ database; Internet site: <http://pdq. state.gov> (accessed 21 October 2003).

[34] White House Fact Sheet: "Joint US-Russia Statement on Trade, Economic Cooperation and Investment," Date: 19940928, PDQ database, Internet site: <http://pdq. state.gov> (accessed 26 November, 2003).

[35] White House Fact Sheet: "Foundation to Support Joint U.S.-NIS Research Efforts," May 1995, Data: 19950510; PDQ database; Internet site: <http://pdq. state.gov> (accessed 10 September 2003).

[36] USIS Washington File: "U.S.-Russia MOU of Understanding on Cultural Exchanges," EPF311 09/02/98; Internet site: <http://usembassy-australia.state.gov/hyper/WF980902/epf311.htm> (accessed 22 December 2003).

in the relationship grew out of various actions on both sides. These burdens on the American-Russian relationship mainly stemmed from three general failures. First, the American political leaders and public had difficulties making the distinction between the downfall of the Soviet Union and the appearance of Russia as the main successor. There was a tendency to treat Russia as a defeated adversary rather than as a forward-looking successor. Undoubtedly, such behavior was one of the reasons why Russian political leaders reacted in a negative way to the United States' claim of supremacy. This, on the other hand, made the American side feel concerned about a so-called neo-liberalism and even Anti-Americanism in Russia. The parliamentary elections in December 1993, when the extreme nationalist Vladimir Zhirinovsky gained political influence in the State Duma (the lower house of the Federal Assembly), left the West in despair.

Second, the well-intended economic support was laid too heavily into the hands of the international community, namely the International Monetary Fund (IMF) and the World Bank. While the U.S. throughout the 1990s followed a policy of supporting large-scale IMF loans to help Russia make a transition to a market economy, only a small amount of direct help had been transferred to Russia. In addition, over these years, there was a shift in assistance from Russia to the other successor states, in particular the Ukraine and Armenia. Whereas the Ukraine by this time had agreed to give up its nuclear weapons and belatedly embarked on economic reform, Russian-American friction had risen and Russia was thought to be less dedicated to reform. A major constraining factor has been the uneven development within Russia's internal political institutions under Yeltsin. Moreover, the Russian government was not able to prevent a worsening of the country's economic situation and the Ruble crashed in October 1994.

This situation caused the U.S. to curtail its export to Russia. Besides the growing U.S. tendency to assume that it would lead and Russia would follow in international relations, the lack of economic growth was the main reason that caused many Russians to become disappointed by the "honeymoon" and to conclude that Russia would have to act to defend its own national interests.[37] However, the greatest failure probably was the United States policy initiative to enlarge NATO to the east, giving membership to former Warsaw Pact allies of the Soviet Union and diminishing the non-aligned belt of states between them and Russia. This kind of policy, as Raymond Garthoff observed, engendered wide concern in Russia:

---

[37] Garthoff (1997), cited above, p. 307.

> To many Russians, the renewal of the cold war Western military alliance by absorbing former members of the defunct Warsaw Pact when there is no threat from Russia can only be seen as creating a new threat to Russia…The United States, as the acknowledged leader of NATO and the principal progenitor of NATO expansion, is held responsible.

Garthoff also mentioned that "most Russians did not place this issue at the forefront of their concerns," and the signing in May 1997 of the Founding Act on Relations between Russia and NATO "defused any immediate crisis in relations." Nonetheless, he went on, "it remains a palliative to an undesirable initiative."[38]

The conflict over NATO enlargement led some observers to call the development of U.S.-Russian relations a transformation "from Cold War to Cold Peace".[39] Despite the discrepancies, throughout Yeltsin's presidency the United States and Russia had developed sufficient bonds of mutual interest between themselves to withstand the negative impact of the expansion of NATO. Their relationship can be summed up, in the words of Garthoff, as "a shift to a normal mix of cooperation and competition, collaboration on areas of congruent national interests and reconciliation or acceptance of divergent interests." Relations were "no longer seen as a zero-sum interaction, as in the Cold War."[40]

Putin and the "New Relationship"

When Yeltsin resigned in December 1999, he thrust Vladimir Putin, a relative unknown, into the limelight. For the U.S. government and the American public, then, as in some ways now, it was not possible to assess the extent of the former KGB (Soviet Intelligence Agency) agent's commitment to democracy and free market. The mystery that surrounds Putin as a private person as well as a political leader reflects the uncertainties surrounding Russian foreign policy in general. Robert Legvold, in 2001, raised the question: "Who are the Russians, and where does the country belong – with the West, with China, or somewhere on its own?"[41] Putin's answer to this seems to be a studious effort not to choose.

Russia faces a fundamental question of identity. Once having been a global power, Russia's share of world GDP in 2000 was down to a little bit more

---

[38] Ibid., p. 311.
[39] for a thorough discussion of the impact of NATO enlargement on U.S.-Russian relations, see Stanley R. Sloan, Steve Woehrel: "NATO Enlargement and Russia: From Cold War to Cold Peace?," CRS Report 95-594 S. May 15, 1995.
[40] Garthoff (1997), cited above, p. 311.
[41] Robert Legvold, Russia's Unformed Foreign Policy, in: *Foreign Affairs* 80/5, 2001, p. 62.

than one percent, compared to the United States' approximately 30 percent.[42] Russians find themselves confronted with a permanent, internal threat – the prospect of domestic economic and political failure. However, as Legvold pointed out: "Russians are aware that, for all its weaknesses, Russia matters to others for three reasons: the atom, the veto, and the location."[43] Russia still possesses nuclear arms. It has a right of veto in the United Nations and its large territory is full of energy resources. The country's relationship with, intelligence about and access to key countries in the regions it borders demonstrates its proximity to the sources of potential threats to the United States. For many Russians, it is not easy to admit that their country is not the great global power it used to be before perestroika. That is why Russian politicians seem to be eager to overemphasize the countries importance in the world. The Russian government's official foreign policy strategy, announced in June 2000, refers to Russia as "a great power ... one of the most influential centers of the modern world ...with a... responsibility for maintaining security in the world both on a global and on a regional level."[44]

The new Administration under President George W. Bush had to find the appropriate answer of how to handle U.S.-Russian relations. Legvold noted two different American attitudes: Some argued the United States should leave the Russians to collect themselves. Since the Russians have few countermeasures in the immediate future, these Americans argue, their objections to U.S. policy initiatives, including the development of a national missile defense, should be ignored and Russian misbehavior punished. An alternate opinion called for the United States government to act in a way that ensures that Russia makes the right choices. However, at that moment in time nothing suggested that Washington or the American public was in a mood to embrace an ambitious policy toward Russia. Instead, the U.S.' disengagement from the Russian problem in the last years of the Clinton administration seemed likely to continue.[45]

The terrorist attacks that rocked the United States on September 11, 2001, opened up a new chapter in the country's relation with the outside world and, as strange as it may sound, had a positive effect on U.S.-Russian relations. Putin became the first world leader to speak with Bush after the attacks, and days later pledged wide-ranging support for the American response. This rapid, positive communication was said to have had a powerful impact upon Bush. Shortly after September 11, the Bush Administration has significantly changed its attitude toward Russia, working much more actively with Moscow. The United States

---

[42] Source: World Bank, reported in: Le Monde diplomatique: Atlas der Globalisierung, Berlin, taz Verlags- und Vertriebs GmbH, 2003; pp. 46-47.
[43] Legvold, cited above, p. 63.
[44] quoted in: Legvold, cited above, p. 62.
[45] Legvold, cited above, pp. 71-72.

also curtailed its criticism of the Russian intervention in Chechnya.[46] September 11 has shown that both countries have a common enemy. U.S.-Russian relations soon started to adapt to the new security environment.

Two months after the terrorist attacks, at the summit in Washington, Bush and Putin signed the Joint Statement on a New U.S.-Russian Relationship. Referring to the new security threat, the statement says, "Dealing with these challenges calls for the creation of a new strategic framework to ensure the mutual security of the United States and Russia, and the world community." This major statement was combined with the Joint Statement on New Russian-American Economic Relationship, which confirmed the United States and Russia's determination to "foster a new dynamic in American-Russian economic interaction." In particular, it underscored the mutual commitment to: accelerate Russia's WTO accession negotiations; fight money laundering and the financing of terrorism; cooperate on Caspian Basin oil and gas projects; support the Russian-American Business Dialogue and the Russian-American Banking Dialogue (both already launched at the Genoa Summit in July); promote bilateral trade and investment opportunities; and assist Russian entrepreneurs and financial institutions.[47] Moreover, the two countries agreed to launch the Russian-American Media Entrepreneurship Dialogue to support free and independent private journalism in Russia.[48]

The Washington Summit laid the basis for agreements that followed during the last two years. To intensify cooperation in the fight against transnational organized crime, the two countries signed the Treaty on Mutual Legal Assistance in Criminal Matters in January 2002. In May, at the summit meeting in Moscow, Bush and Putin agreed on a new "Foundation for Cooperation," a new strategic relationship "based on friendship, cooperation, common values, trust, openness, and predictability." The joint declaration contained provisions regarding Russian-American political cooperation in terms of such hotspots as Afghanistan, Central Asia and the South Caucasus. It also covered economic cooperation; the strengthening of people-to-people contacts; the prevention of the spread of weapons of mass destruction; a joint center for the exchange of data from early warning systems and the study of possible areas

---

[46] Paul J. Saunders, U.S.-Russian relations after September 11: A report on the U.S.-Russia Dialogue, The Nixon Center, January 2002; Internet site: <http://www.nixoncenter.og> (accessed 20 September 2003).

[47] The White House Office of the Press Secretary: "Joint Statement on New Russian-American Economic Relationship," November 13, 2001; Internet Site <http://usinfo.state.gov/regional /eur/russia/ economics. htm> (accessed 12 November 2003).

[48] The White House Office of the Press Secretary: "Joint Statement on New U.S.-Russian Relationship," November 13, 2001; Internet Site: <http://www.whitehouse.gov/news/releases /2001/11/20011113-4. html> (accessed 26 November 2003).

of missile defense cooperation. In addition, an Energy Dialogue was launched and a treaty on further reduction of strategic nuclear warheads was signed.[49]

Also in May, the NATO-Russia Council was established in Rome. It represented the beginning of a new era in NATO-Russia relations through a new level of Russian involvement in European security. Although Moscow and Washington had their tense periods over NATO intervention in Yugoslavia in 1994 and 1995, Timothy J. Colton and Michael McFaul, in 2001, remarked: U.S. and Russian militaries now serve side by side in Bosnia and Kosovo. Neither NATO enlargement in Eastern Europe nor the alliance's intervention in Yugoslavia – both which were bitterly resisted by Moscow – have sidetracked this new relationship.[50]

Although there had been such far-reaching steps of approach since September 11, the conflict of Iraq in the middle of the following year seemed to conclude an entire epoch in American-Russian relations. In early 2003, Russia used its veto in the United Nations Security Council to hinder the U.S from military actions against Iraq. This, along with an unprecedented amount of anti-Americanism in Russian society, was the reason Washington and the American public stopped looking at Russia as an ally and partner. Given Russia's promising reaction to America's shock over September 11, this recent disappointment has clearly been more painful. The short-lived image of Russia as a serious future strategic partner had disappeared.[51] Nonetheless, in June 2003, shortly after the U.S. troops marched into Iraq, Bush met Putin in St.Petersburg to congratulate him on the anniversary of his native city. Hence, at least on the government-to-government level, both sides acted as if the recent sparring over Iraq had not hurt the fundamental partnership. It gave the impression that all was well in the relationship of the two countries. The main reason for this kind of behavior is simple: The interests America and Russia share greatly outweigh the interests that divide them.

Many voices, however, call for a review of the U.S.-Russian relationship. While there are those who think that the U.S. should "punish" Russia for its disloyalty, other voices call for a more innovative approach. The Commission

---

[49] The White House Office of Press Secretary: "Joint Declaration on New US-Russia Relationship," Date: 20020524; Internet Site: <http://www.whitehouse.gov/news/releases/2001/11/20011113-4. html> (accessed 26 November 2003).
[50] Timothy J. Colton, Michael McFaul, America's real Russian Allies, in *Foreign Affairs* 80/6, 2001, p. 48.
[51] Nikolai V. Zlobin, "Disappointment Replaces Friendship", Diplomatic Courier, article taken and translated from *Nezavisimaya Gazeta*, May 26, 2003; Internet Site: <http://www.cdi.org/zlobin/ disappointment.cfm> (accessed 12 October 2003).

on America's National Interests and Russia[52], for example, in an Interim Report issued in September 2003, argued:

> ... as the Iraq experience demonstrates, changes in the format and style of communications with Russia are necessary ... Communication with Russia is complicated by Russian unrealistic expectation of symmetry that have not yet fully accommodated very real asymmetries in the bilateral relationship...the Bush Administration must take a series of steps to improve counter-terrorism cooperation ... U.S. leaders should recognize that economic modernization is Russia's number one national priority. ...Moreover, if Russia cooperates in stabilizing post-war Iraq, the U.S. should be 'imaginative' in honoring Russian interest there.[53]

Among the most difficult issues of U.S.-Russian relations are Iraq, Iran and North Korea. The historical experiences of the United States and Russia with each of these countries are very different. It is not surprising to find differences in outlook. Most importantly, each of these issues appears to be the subject of complex but productive dialogue.

---

[52] The Commission on America's National Interests and Russia is an outgrowth of the Commission on America's National Interest. The current commission addresses the specific issue of American national interests and Russia.

[53] The Commission on America's National Interests and Russia Executive, "Advancing American Interests and the U.S.-Russian Relationship" – Interim Report, Washington, D.C., September 2003; Internet Site: <http://www.nixoncenter.org/publications/Program%20Briefs/interim% 20report %20final%20complete. pdf >(accessed 9 November 2003).

3. U.S. Assistance to Russia[54]

Throughout the Cold War years, the possibility of providing the Soviet Union with what is commonly considered foreign aid (grant or concessional assistance) rarely surfaced as an issue in U.S. politics. The U.S. Administrations provided few direct economic aid grants, concessional loans or other benefits to their chief rival. On a few occasions, the U.S. provided emergency disaster assistance, as in the case of the Chernobyl nuclear disaster. Gorbachev's rise to Soviet leadership in 1985 and his subsequent efforts to introduce sweeping political and economic reforms brought about U.S. support for closer bilateral economic relations. The Bush Administration was very reluctant to provide assistance because the Soviet Union was still viewed with suspicion and foreign aid was seen as a gift. The only important concession made was in 1987 when the Soviet Union gained access to subsidies of U.S. wheat purchases. In mid 1990, Gorbachev, for the first time, directly appealed for U.S. and western food and medical assistance. Whereas European governments moved quickly to provide assistance to the Soviets (with Germany taking the lead) in the United States debate continued through much of 1990 over whether, how and under what conditions the United States should assist Moscow.

It was not until the rise of a democratic movement led by Boris Yeltsin after the attempted coup of August 1991 that U.S. policymakers began to talk about large levels of assistance. Bush, consistent with his policy of caution, resisted the calls for higher amounts of assistance to democratic forces in the Soviet Union and he was perceived as being slow to respond to the new wave of events there. However, when several Members of Congress argued that provision of assistance was in the United States national interest, they successfully won approval of assistance to help the Soviet Union dismantle nuclear weapons, an effort which became known as the Nunn-Lugar program.[55] Nonetheless, this did not cause the Bush Administration to develop its own initiatives. Although Gorbachev had already asked the U.S. for another credit to purchase grain, Bush did not see any reason for immediate action. Instead, he assured worried journalists that "Nobody is going to starve."[56]

One possible reason for the Bush Administration's reserved standpoint was an anti-foreign policy trend among the U.S. electorate. Both, Democrats and Republicans criticized Bush for spending too much of his time on foreign affairs to the detriment of the U.S. economy. The Republicans around Pat Buchanan,

---

[54] With regard to Russian assistance, the chapter will only focus on direct U.S. funds to Russia, and leave aside indirect U.S. support through IMF and World Bank credits to Russia.

[55] Curt Tamoff, "U.S. Assistance to the Former Soviet Union 1991-2001: A History of Administration and Congressional Action", CRS Report for Congress, Order Code RL30148, updated January 15, 2002, pp. 2-6.

[56] quoted in: Andrew Rosenthal, "$ 1 Billion Credit to Soviets Urged", *New York Times*, October 23, 1991, A6.

for example, attacked him with *America-first* slogans. Just prior to the dissolution of the Soviet Union, however, the Bush Administration came forward with a proposal for the first significant assistance package which aimed to comply with Gorbachev's wishes, appease the Europeans and soothe the American agricultural lobby. At the end, in November 1991, the Congress passed an assistance package of a modest $500 million, with the largest part ($ 400 million) intended to assist demilitarization measures like the dismantling of nuclear weapons. With the remaining amount of $100 million the United States, for the first time in 70 years, would supply free of charge food to the Soviet Union. The decision marked a step forward toward a more active assistance policy of the Bush Administration.[57]

In 1992, the aid debate focused on the Freedom Support Act, the Bush Administration's proposal that laid out the basic authorities, conditions and guidelines for humanitarian assistance, technical assistance and assistance for broadened educational and cultural exchange. When Yeltsin, during the summit meeting in Washington and Camp David from June 16-18, made wide-ranging concessions with regard to arms reduction, meaning a de facto abandoning of the strategic parity, a positive mood was triggered within the public and Congress. What finally backed up the proponents of Russian assistance was a CBS/NYT poll, conducted from June 17-20, which showed a majority of 49 percent of Americans being for a U.S. participation in financial assistance to Russia. Just two weeks before, a survey conducted by NBC/Wall Street Journal found 51 percent of the respondents opposed financial support for Russia. Hence, it is not surprising that the Freedom Support Act became law soon afterwards, on October 24. It constituted the basis for direct U.S. assistance to Russia in the forthcoming years.[58]

Doubtless, the launching of the Freedom Support Program was a move that led to the first wide-ranging direct U.S. economic assistance since the dissolution of the Soviet Union. (In 1992, the United States share of all Western economic aid was only about 10 percent, in contrast to Germany's 60 percent.)[59] The Program established the basis for America's ability to influence the transformation of Russia's political and economical system. Although the initial sum appropriated (about $ 400 million) was quite modest, the program was a landmark in American-Russian relations. The Bush Administration, for the first time, had acted without hesitation and the United States since then would play a leading role in assistance to Moscow.[60]

---

[57] Stephan G. Bierling, *Wirtschaftshilfe für Moskau: Motive und Strategien der Bundesrepublik Deutschland und der USA 1990-1996*, Paderborn, Ferdinand Schöningh, 1998, pp. 176-178.
[58] Ibid., pp. 189-191.
[59] Garthoff (1997), cited above, p. 308.
[60] Bierling, cited above, pp. 191-192, 235.

At the beginning of 1993, the economic and political status of Russia had become increasingly precarious. Many observers feared that social unrest could endanger the entire venture into a market economy and argued that increased U.S. aid would be necessary. The crux of their view was that the economic and political stability of the region was of vital importance to American interests. The new Clinton administration in this atmosphere proposed a dramatic increase in the amount of funding and several new priorities for the program, mainly with the purpose to more effectively support Russia's transition toward a market economy and democracy. By 1994, a mix of concerns emerged regarding the U.S. budget deficit, the unpromising outcome of the December 1993 Russian parliamentary elections (see earlier in this chapter) and critical questions about the implementation of the assistance program. This led to efforts to cut funding for the NIS region. These concerns altered existing priorities, especially by shifting funds from Russia to other successor states like Ukraine, Armenia, and Georgia. In 1995, the new Republican majority in Congress cut funds to the region with Russia being a particular target of these cuts.[61]

From 1992 through 1997, the U.S. government obliged $4.5 billion in grant assistance to Russia, including $2.1 billion in Freedom Support Act aid for market reform and democratization and $857 million for Cooperative Threat Reduction (Nunn-Lugar assistance). Even so, Russia's share of the shrinking NIS foreign aid account fell from about 60 percent in 1993-1994 to roughly 17 percent in 1998. In 1997, the Clinton Administration launched the Partnership for Freedom (PFF) initiative, which sought to reverse these downward trends, but Congress rejected the proposed increases in Russian and NIS aid. The Administration attempted again to obtain more funding for Russia programs in 1998. In the end, Russia was allocated $172 million for 1999, a 29 percent increase over the previous year and 20 percent of the 1999 NIS account.[62] Since then, the funding for Russia again has declined. While the funds in 2003 represented nearly 19 percent of NIS allocations, the Administration's request for 2004 is $73 million, 13 percent of the total NIS account. This profoundly diminished Administration request - a 48% cut - indicates a plan to "graduate" Russia from the aid program over the next few years.[63] All in all, the amounts and favorable consequences of American assistance throughout the nineties was far from what Russia had counted on and fell short of even the most cautious expectations.[64]

---

[61] Tamoff, cited above, pp. 11-25.
[62] Stuart D. Goldman, "Russia", CRS Report for Congress, Order Code IB92089, June 15, 2000.
[63] Curt Tarnoff, The Former Soviet Union and U.S. Foreign Assistance, CRS Issue Brief for Congress, Order Code IB95077, updated September 16, 2003, pp. 9-10; Internet Site: <http://www.usembassy.it/ pdf/other/IB95077.pdf> (accessed 20 November 2003).
[64] Eric Shiraev, Vladislav Zubok, *Anti-Americanism in Russia*, New York, Palgrave, 2000, p. 52.

There are a number of reasons for the historic decline in Russian aid. One reason, possibly, was the declining public support. In general, foreign aid is less accepted in the United States than in most of the other western countries. According to Organization for Economic Cooperation and Development (OECD) statistical data of 2001, the United States, with roughly 0.1 percent of its GDP, helps foreign countries less than all other members of the OECD.[65] Although Bush, and later Clinton, for a short time, managed to convince majorities in Congress and in the public that Russia aid serves U.S. interests, the readiness to continue the support diminished again. With Russia no longer being a direct threat, the atmosphere of urgency for aid was missing. In the June 2002 CCFR poll (a year when Russia aid already was on a very low level) only 16 percent wanted to increase spending in aid to Russia. Forty-six percent wanted to maintain current spending levels, while 33 percent wanted to either decrease current levels (17%) or stop aid altogether (15%).[66] In the political debate, other reasons were given for the decline of Russia aid. While some argued in the past that more of the NIS account should be funneled to other countries in the region, which had shown progress in democratization and the establishment of a market economy, others criticized Russian domestic and international behavior and either sought cuts in aid or sought to use the aid program as leverage in changing Russian behavior.

Although a variety of conditions have been proposed by Congressmen, three conditions in particular have become a regular focus of debate since 1995: the sale of nuclear reactors to Iran, Russian behavior in Chechnya, and implementation of a law regulating religious minorities. Moreover, the Freedom Support Act and annual foreign operations appropriations bills contain general conditions that all states of the former Soviet Union are expected to meet in order to receive assistance. The conditions for Russia (as for all the other successor states) include whether it is undertaking economic and political reform. Economic assistance, as a rule, is provided to reach political goals. Financial support to Russia was no exception. Besides other U.S. interests in Russia, the major political goals for the United States were first, to be able to control the dismantling of the former Soviet Union's nuclear arsenal, second, to influence the developments within Russia, and third, to have an effect on Moscow's foreign policy in the long run. While Russia's military capacities today do not constitute a direct threat to the U.S. anymore, the expectations with regard to the latter two goals turned out to be an illusion.

---

[65] Source: OECD, in: Le Monde diplomatique: Atlas der Globalisierung, Berlin, taz Verlags- und Vertriebs GmbH, 2003, p. 51.

[66] reported in: PIPA, "Americans and the World," Public Opinion on International Affairs, Report: Americans on Russia (last revised November 22, 2002); Internet site: <http://www.americans-world.org/digest/ regional_issues/russia/summary.cfm> (accessed 10 September 2003).

4. Russia's "Incomplete" Transformation

> *Russia is predictable in the sense that*
> *it will continue to be unpredictable.*

-- Marshall Goldman[67]

While the Bush Administration today argues that it is time for Russia to "graduate" from democracy assistance, presumably on the grounds that Russia is now a democracy and has succeeded in implementing a market economy, supporters of a larger aid program argue that democracy is by no means assured and economic reforms remain incomplete.[68] How close did Russia come to fulfilling the definition of a national friend with "similar values, policies, and goals" given by the respondents of the "Friends and Enemies" project? Did the country develop into a democratic country? Did and does it "agree with U.S. views," which are "procapitalist" and "anticommunist"? Finally, did Russia "take U.S advice" and did it "comply with U.S. wishes"?

Before Gorbachev appeared in the limelight with his new ideas of economic "restructuring" (*perestroika*), public "openness" (*glasnost'*)[69], and "democratization" (*democratizatsia*) there was not a single sign, since Khrushchev's partial de-Stalinization and liberalization in the 1960s, that indicated Moscow's willingness to change anything in the system of dictatorship nor to remove the inherent barriers against freedom of speech. Both societies could not have been more different, with market economy, capitalism and democracy on the one hand and planned economy, communism and dictatorship on the other. They were the primary ideological foes in a bipolar world for more than forty years.

The New "Openness"

Through "*glasnost'*," Gorbachev opened what Joseph S. Nye, Jr. called a "black box", referring to the closed nature of the Soviet society with Soviet intentions remaining largely opaque.[70] For Americans this meant that they gained better information about the Soviet Union, that the Soviet regime became less secretive

---

[67] quoted in: Leontovitsh, O.A.: *Russkie i Amerikantsy: Paradoksy Mezhkul'turnovo Obshtshenia* (Russians and Americans: Paradoxes of Cross-Cultural Communication), Volgograd, Peremena, 2002, p. 190.

[68] „Potemkin Democracy", Washington Post, May 30, 2003, Editorial, A22.

[69] In fact, the closest meaning in English is "publicity", "public airing", or "open debate" of issues and problems. There is an entirely different Russian word "*otkrovennost'*," meaning openness.

[70] Joseph S. Nye Jr., Gorbachev's Russia and U.S. Options, in: *Gorbachev's Russia and American Foreign Policy*, Seweryn Bialer, Michael Mandelbaum (eds.), Bolder, London, Westview Press, 1988, p. 386.

in their eyes and that many lost their "over-simplified and emotionally colored stereotypes"[71] of the Russians. For Russians the concept of "*glasnost*'" under Gorbachev was a refreshing policy, which in William H. Luers words "has made possible the discussion, with official sanctions, of the sources of weakness and stagnation of the Soviet system, making possible creative responses to them." Luers stated that it was "an important and powerful phenomenon in a closed society," but in 1988 observed that:

> ...it is not 'openness' as Westerners...conceive of the term. Some foreign radio broadcasts to the Soviet Union are still jammed; foreign travel and emigration is still severely restricted; hundreds, if not thousands of prisoners of conscience are still in prisons, labor camps and in internal exile; the KGB is still performing surveillance; the borders are still heavily armed, tourists followed, trade seriously restricted, and data still concealed. An open debate and 'airing' is not 'openness'[72]

Nonetheless, it was an important first step that finally led to the end of censorship and a much more open society where Russians would be able to practice freedom of speech. These constitutional rights were established in the 29th Article of Russia's new constitution in December 1993. The constitution also guarantees freedom of the press. However, American and other western observers became increasingly concerned with Russia's lack of a free press. Lee S. Wolosky, in 2000, argued that the problem was "not because of government censorship but because of oligarch control of the most meaningful media outlets."[73] Later, when Putin and his surrogates eliminated the biggest independent media groups under Boris Berezovsky and Vladimir Gussinsky, the most important Russian media moguls at the time, other American observers thought that such a behavior "vividly demonstrated Putin's intolerance of journalists who dare to criticize him."[74]

The Economic Transformation

With "*perestroika*", Gorbachev revised "the notion of an economy centrally planned by all-knowing authorities, in favor of greater local autonomy, incentives and, over time, market forces."[75] Graham T. Allison, in 1988, vividly described the disastrous economic situation Gorbachev was confronted with after his succession:

---

[71] Marshal D. Shulman referred to the stereotypes that during the Cold War have exacerbated American reactions to Soviet behaviour and vice versa. quoted in: Nye Jr., cited above, p. 401.

[72] William H. Luers, U.S. Policy and Gorbachev's Russia, in: *Gorbachev's Russia and American Foreign Policy*, Seweryn Bialer, Michael Mandelbaum (eds.), Bolder, London, Westview Press, 1988, p. 414.

[73] Lee S. Wolosky, Putin's Plutocrat Problem, in: *Foreign Affairs* 79/2, 2000, p. 28.

[74] Colton, McFaul, cited above, p. 50.

[75] Allison, cited above, p. 20.

Gorbachev is the first Soviet leader to understand the failure of the socialist economic system. That failure is evident in an economy that achieved five-percent growth in the 1960s, fell to two-percent growth in the first half of the 1970s, and stagnated at virtually zero growth by the early 1980s. Failure is evident in a military that now consumes at least 15-20 percent of the nation's product but cannot prevent a Cessna 172 from landing in Red Square, and allows Afghan rebels to defeat the mighty Red Army. Failure is evident in a health care system that alone among those of industrial nations has seen *reductions* in average life expectancy. It is evident in a technological base that still has not produced a personal computer for general consumption, when countries such as Taiwan and South Korea manage to market second- and third-generation personal computers around the world.[76]

Hence, shortly after Gorbachev took office it became clear that the Soviet Union's system of planned economy had failed. But since then, to what extent did the economic reforms initiated by Gorbachev transform Russia's economy? Throughout the 1990s, the American media produced a false picture of Russia as being on its way to full recovery. Stephen F. Cohen described the reason for this "bleak chapter in the history of American journalism" as follows:

Underlying all the American misreporting and false analyses of the nineties was an enthusiastic embrace of the Clinton Administration's ill-conceived policy – a virtual crusade to transform post-Communist Russia under President Boris Yeltsin into a replica of America through U.S.-sponsored 'reforms,' first and foremost economic 'shock therapy.' The crusade was (and remains) an official project, but it also captivated investors, academics and journalists, who in their respective professional (or unprofessional) ways became its missionaries.[77]

According to a 1996 survey, Moscow correspondents tended to look at events in Russia "through the prism of their own expectations and beliefs."[78] Cohen likens this behavior to the American journalistic malpractice during the 1917 Revolution in Russia. U.S. correspondents, according to an analysis by Walter Lippmann and Charles Merz, strongly believed in their government's anti-Red crusade and had thus seen "not what was, but what men wished to see." Cohen went on, complaining that "there had been no media (or official) reconsideration of the arrogant, intrusive and dangerously counterproductive U.S. crusade to transform a different civilization." He cited the Washington Post's chief Moscow correspondent (David Hoffman), who in late 1999 extolled "the Russian transition," marveling that "Russians have accomplished much of what

---

[76] Ibid., p. 20.
[77] Stephen F. Cohen, American Journalism and Russia's Tragedy, in: *The Nation*, Oct. 2, 2000.
[78] Ellen Shearer, Frank Starr: Through a Prism Darkly, in: *American Journalism Review*, Sept. 1996, p. 37.

we asked." In reality, the prescriptions, reports and prognoses that many of America's professional Russia-watchers (policy-makers, financial advisers, scholars, and journalists) made at the beginning of the so-called shock-therapy "have turned out to be completely wrong." Cohen, in late 2000, came to the following conclusion:

> Nearly a decade later, Russia is afflicted by the worst economic depression in modern history, corruption so extensive that capital flight far exceeds all foreign loans and investment, and a demographic catastrophe unprecedented in peacetime. The result has been a massive human tragedy. Among other calamities, some 75 percent of Russians now live below or barely above the poverty line; 50-80 percent of school-age children are classified as having a physical or mental defect; and male life expectancy has plunged to less then sixty years.[79]

Furthermore, Cohen pointed out, in the American media the "Great Transition Depression," as a UN study[80] called it at the end of the 1990s, was almost never mentioned.

Although the economic reforms suffered many setbacks and disappointments, most observers at the end of the decade believed they "carried Russia beyond the point of no return as far as restoring the old Soviet system is concerned."[81] However flawed, a market economy had been created. On June 6, 2002, Washington formally declared Russia a market economy. The Department of Commerce (DOC), which granted this status in the quasi-judicial process before the declaration, emphasized:

> Russian economic conditions have changed so dramatically over the past decade, and the role of the government in the economy has declined so substantially over that time period, that the country has long been operating as a market economy. ... As the Department repeatedly has recognized in prior market economy determinations, there is no absolute standard by which the market economy designation may be determined; perfect *laissez-faire* capitalism is neither attainable nor required. ... Although we envision the United States as the paradigmatic example of a market economy, its specific features and conditions are not determinative of the status of other countries.[82]

---

[79] Cohen, cited above.

[80] Human Development Report for Central and Eastern Europe and the CIS 1999, New York, 1999, p. 15.

[81] Goldman, cited above.

[82] U.S. Department of Commerce: Before the International Trade Administration; Case No. A-821-816; In the matter of: The status of the Russian Federation as a non-market economy country under the antidumping and counter veiling duty laws, pp. 2-4; Internet Site: <http://ia.ita.doc.gov/download/ russia-nme-status/posthearing/powell-goldstein/russian-producers-040802.pdf> (accessed 24 November 2003).

In the same document the Department of Commerce justified its standpoint by listing the statutory criteria for determining Russia's status as a market economy. The most important of these criteria were "the extent of the convertibility of the Russian Ruble," "the extent to which wage rates are determined by free bargaining between labor and management," "the extent to which joint ventures and foreign investment are permitted in Russia" and "the extent to which the Russian government retains ownership or control of the means of production." The Carnegie Endowment for International Peace in late 2000 found:

> More than two-thirds of Russia's GDP is now produced by the private sector...Russia returned to economic growth in 1999, and the significant growth may well continue. The country has accomplished macroeconomic stabilization, inflation has been brought under control, and the Russian national budget has been balanced.[83]

For the most part, these encouraging developments are the result of artificial and temporary factors. Thanks to high oil prices and the substantial devaluation of 1998, Russia enjoys a sizable trade and current account surplus. Russia's economic weakness is still manifest. The market designation, as William Corley concluded after the DOC decision, "is rather technical and will primarily affect future anti-dumping investigations." He went on in arguing that this is but a small step in Russia's integration into the global economy and pointed out:

> Much remains to be done in Russia. Critics cite corruption, bureaucracy, and lack of transparency and rule of law as some of the many reasons why Russia does not belong – or is incapable of functioning well – in the world economy ... accounting for less than two percent of global merchandise trade ... However, change is in the air. It remains to be seen in this decade just how far Russia will go in reforming itself, developing its economy...[84]

Many American Russia-observers agree that Putin, on economics, has assembled the most pro-reform team since the beginning of the 1990s and has pushed through some ambitious market-oriented reforms. This set of reform measures presumably gave further strength to the economy, which by early 2000 started to recover from the 1998 crisis. This positive trend led the Carnegie Endowment of International Peace to call for a decrease of economic aid to

[83] Carnegie Endowment for International Peace, An Agenda for Renewal – A Report by the Russian and Eurasian Program of the Carnegie Endowment for International Peace, 2000, p. 44; Internet Site: <http://www.carnegie.ru/en/pubs/books/ 2132FullTextEng.pdf> (accessed 20 October 2003).

[84] William Corley, Milestones in U.S.-Russian History – Market Economy Status, and a Little Respect, for Russia, in: *Export America* July 2002, pp. 10-11.

Russia, with the argument that most economic assistance programs were no longer necessary.

The Road to an Unstable Democracy

By contrast, the endowment stated that, "democracy assistance programs are as necessary today as at any time in Russia's post-Soviet history" and suggested that funds for economic development should rather be shifted to democracy aid:

> Over the course of the last decade, democracy promotion has been a distant fourth on the list of U.S. assistance priorities vis-á-vis Russia, after denuclearization, economic reform, and humanitarian projects. These three areas constituted $ 4.48 billion of the $ 5.45 billion in total assistance for Russia from the U.S. government from 1992 to 1998. Of that $ 5.45 billion, only $ 130 million (2.3 percent) was devoted to programs directly aimed at advancing democracy.

According to this Russia-observer, Putin, while progressive with regard to economic reforms, "is centralizing power and weakening Russia's already shaky democratic institutions."[85] Colton and McFaul in 2001 pointed out that:

> Russia's transition from authoritarianism is far from complete ... As preoccupied as Washington is with its new campaign against terrorism, inattention to the fragility of Russian democracy would be a huge mistake – and one that could have serious negative consequences for American security. Now is the time for the United States to redouble its efforts to promote democracy within the borders of its former adversary.[86]

This implies that Russia, more than a decade after Gorbachev declared "*democratizatia*" a goal of his reforms, is far from being a stable, deep-rooted democracy. The visions of the supporters of increased U.S. democracy assistance, however, did not materialize. As mentioned earlier in this chapter, the Bush Administration even plans to "graduate" Russia from the current aid program.

If not completely, then, how and to what extent did Russia develop toward a democracy? Under Gorbachev, democratization was very limited. For example, only a few percent of the June 1987 local elections involved more than one candidate.[87] In 1991, Allison and Blackwill pointed out that although Gorbachev expressed appreciation for Western values of freedom and democracy, he nonetheless was a communist: "... as westerners romanticize this Russian leader, they should recall that Gorbachev grew up under communism,

---

[85] Carnegie Endowment for International Peace, cited above, pp. 37, iv.

[86] Colton, McFaul, cited above, p. 47.

[87] Nye, Jr., cited above, p. 403.

rose to power through the party's ranks and continues to pledge his allegiance to communism."[88]

In December 1993, Russia's new constitution provided for a parliamentary system with an ordinary division of power between a strong executive, and a parliament reduced to a legislative role. However, Russia's political system is not a parliamentary-presidential system as, for example, the one in Poland, where the balance of power tends to shift in favor of the parliament. It is instead a presidential-parliamentary system, where the president has stronger prerogatives to compete with the legislative and executive branches. Yeltsin vividly demonstrated this power when he regularly fired his ministers and repeatedly threatened to dissolve the parliament. While Clinton continued to express satisfaction with Russia's democratic progress during the January 1994 summit in Moscow, Yeltsin's behavior caused Zbigniew Brzezinski to come to a very pessimistic conclusion with regard to Russia's transformation toward a democracy:

> Unfortunately, considerable evidence suggests that the near-term prospects for a stable Russian democracy are not very promising ... President Yeltsin's inclination toward authoritarianism has transformed the new constitution for a democratic Russia into a document that can be easily used to legitimize arbitrary personal rule. Russian political culture is still far from accepting the principle of compromise as the basis for political discourse.[89]

Neutral western observers of Russia's political system also found that the kind of uncontrolled executive and legislative accumulation of power in the hands of the Russian president results in a low level of transparency and a missing effective control of the decision making power of the president. This, in turn, leads to problematic democracy deficiencies.[90]

Interestingly, Russia's political system with regard to some aspects is very similar to the American presidential system. The Russian president is directly elected for a period of four years. While he can veto parliamentary decisions, the parliament can impeach him. However, the Russian president holds a range of power, which largely exceeds that of the American president. The Russian president has the right to dissolve the parliament and does not rely as heavily on the legislative process as his American counterpart. Many American observers perceive an uncertain democratic character of Russia's current president and former KGB colonel, Putin. They see his efforts to centralize power by weakening the regional governors, and all major sources of power independent

---

[88] Allison, Blackwill, cited above, p. 80.
[89] Zbigniew Brzezinski, The Premature Partnership, in: *Foreign Affairs* 73/2, 1994, pp. 71-72.
[90] Margareta Mommsen, Das ‚System Jelzin" – Struktur und Funktionsweise des russischen „Superpräsidentialismus", in: *Demokratie in Ost und West*. Festschrift für Klaus von Beyme, Wolfgang Merkel, Andreas Busch (eds.). Franfurt a.M., 1999, p. 293.

of the executive branch. His attacks on independent media, his challenges to Russia's business oligarchs, and his indifference to human rights in Chechnya are a bone of contention. A report of the Russian and Eurasian program of the Carnegie Endowment for International Peace from late 2000 reads: "If Russia was a wobbly democracy under President Yeltsin, it is now in the gray zone between democracy and authoritarianism. The timing and likely direction of its exit from the gray zone will become evident only once Putin makes clear what political lines he will draw."[91]

The situation has not changed since then. Although not all of Putin's reforms have been antidemocratic, like the legal reform and his economic policies, Colton and McFaul in late 2001, emphasized that, "ever since Putin came to power, Russia has by and large grown less democratic." The two Russia observers found that "the State Security Service (the former KGB) has stepped up its harassment of investigative journalists, human rights activists, environmental leaders and Western nongovernmental organizations (NGOs) and religious groups, along with their Russian affiliates." Colton and McFaul also mentioned polling data, which testify that only 20 percent of Russians categorized their state as a democracy and that most still lamented the dismantling of the Soviet Union in 1991.[92] Moreover, the Communist Party, under Gennady Zyuganov, still enjoys considerable popularity in the Russian electorate. The 2000 report of the Carnegie Endowment emphasized:

> Russians' perceptions of their country and their relationship with the United States are often at odds with American's understanding. Whereas American observers automatically assume democracy and market economics to be good things, these terms ring false to many Russians. Uncritical talk of 'reforms,' 'democracy,' 'markets,' and 'capitalism' in Russia provokes disgust among many Russians, based on the punishing realities around them – powerful elites who seem to run the country only for their own benefit, rising inequality throughout the society, increased crime, social instability, and economic hardship for many ordinary people.[93]

According to a survey, the report goes on, a large majority of Russians (71%) still had a positive attitude toward the political system before perestroika, and a majority of 48 percent had a negative attitude to the present system of government. Interestingly, however, a large majority of 67 percent generally agreed with the statement "Our country ought to be democratic." This implies that Russian citizens may be unhappy with the way their national institutions work, but the majority of them robustly support democratic norms. The Carnegie Endowment for International Peace, in its report wisely concluded:

---

[91] Carnegie Endowment for International Peace, cited above, p. 3.

[92] Colton, McFaul, cited above, p. 50.

[93] Carnegie Endowment for International Peace, cited above, p. 6.

"As much as Americans may prefer to divide up the world into black and white categories, Russia cannot be so pigeonholed. Real cooperation is possible between the United States and Russia, but the relationship must not be driven by exaggerated expectations of either a positive or negative variety."[94]

Russian Anti-Americanism

It is no secret that in recent years a so-called "new" anti-Americanism has been observed in considerable parts of Russian society. It is new in the sense that it differs from the "old" Soviet anti-Americanism, which was ideology-driven and the product of decades of Cold War confrontation, but represented a rather superficial state of mind. While the Soviet government made every effort to spread Communist and anti-American propaganda, the Russian people adopted largely neutral and even friendly attitudes toward Americans. It was, therefore, no surprise when the "old" anti-Americanism collapsed along with Communist rule. The nineties, however, witnessed a rise of negative opinion when public attitudes toward the United States changed from admiration and hope to suspiciousness and alienation. Eric Shiraev and Vladislav Zubok in their thorough study of anti-Americanism in Russia found three major forming factors of the new anti-American sentiment:

> The first, was the extraordinarily long and deep economic depression of the 1990s and, as a result, the demise of public belief in macroeconomic solutions, private property and, to an extent, in liberal Democracy. The second, was the search for a new national Russian identity that brought to the fore some well-articulated strands of nationalism, isolationism, and anti-Western sentiment that had previously been on the margins of Russian public knowledge. The third, was Russia's new democratic politics that, along with the pluralism of opinion and the growth of mutual tolerance, led to the emergence of the anti-American "card" in factional and electoral strategies.[95]

A growing number of Russian opinion-makers spread their anti-American views throughout the public. One of these views was that America wanted to keep Russia weak by opposing any attempt to extend its influence to the other former Soviet republics. Another wide-spread opinion was that the U.S. was the country that benefited most from the collapse of the Soviet Union. Some voices argued that America hindered Russia from being in a position to compete economically and blamed the U.S. for the refusal to give Russia most favored nation trade status and provide any serious financial help. The irritation caused by the American "helpers," according to Shiraev and Zubok "peaked right after the

---

[94] Ibid., pp. 4-7.

[95] Shiraev, Zubok, cited above, p. 3.

financial crash of August 1998, a crisis that had a profoundly sobering effect on the entire Russian society." While by 1993, anti-American attitudes were shared by approximately 30-40 percent of Russians, public opinion polls at the end of the nineties yielded a steady 60-70 percent level of anti-American sentiment.[96] Americans were increasingly perceived as arrogant "teachers." As Shiraev and Zubok observed, "Russians clearly showed that they did not like to be lectured on right and wrong behavior, especially when the lecturers failed to make a positive change in people's lives. Moreover – in the eyes of many people – the mentors from overseas made their lives worse."[97]

After the terrorist attacks that rocked the United States on September 11, Moscow pledged wide-ranging support for the American response, and a great many Russians expressed sympathy with Americans. A Russian poll at that time, found 85 percent of Muscovites felt that the attacks were aimed not only at the United States, but at all of mankind.[98] However, as the war in Iraq was beginning, Putin strongly criticized the U.S.-led operations as unjustifiable and a bad mistake. Interestingly, his tone has changed dramatically just two weeks later, taking a pragmatic approach to relations with the U.S. by emphasizing the importance of economic and trade ties with America. Masha Lipman, a Russian journalist, who writes a monthly column for the *Washington Post*, concluded that this was a "tricky balancing act" and observed:

> On the one hand, Putin seems to be fully determined to integrate Russia into the world economy....Yet on the other hand, the Russian president has to deal with anti-American sentiment among the public and parts of the elite. The public may remain relatively passive – there have been no street protests to speak of – but polls show strong antiwar, or anti-American, feelings. Never under Putin's rule has the percentage of Russians taking a negative attitude toward America been so high.[99]

Lipman argues that the new anti-Americanism in Russia is not very deep because it does not stem from any "profound cultural hostility but rather from frustration over the loss of superpower parity with the United States." Nevertheless, the views of Americans and Russians on an issue of global importance have separated once more and the new anti-American feelings in Russia will not subside anytime soon.

---

[96] Ibid., pp. 145, 147.
[97] Ibid., pp. 53, 56.
[98] Colton, McFaul, cited above, p. 47.
[99] Masha Lipman, "Russia's Politics of Anti-Americanism," *Washington Post*, April 6, 2003; p. B07.

II THE CHANGING AMERICAN PERCEPTION OF RUSSIA

Each side imagines that it faces an inherently,
implacably aggressive enemy when actually
it faces an enemy as fearful as itself.

-- Ralph K. White (1984)[100]

Americans and Russians need not love one another and they are
unlikely to become allies anytime soon. Meanwhile, it will be enough
if they understand that they need each other, that they need
to cooperate with one another... Much is possible if we
look at things realistically and set realistic goals.

-- Georgi Arbatov (1996)[101]

5. The American Mind

To find out if Americans perceive another nation as enemy or ally one has to look at the outcomes of public opinion surveys,[102] polls that show a representative picture of the "average" American attitude. The expression "public opinion", as such, refers to the notion that a large number of people in a country are thinking along certain common lines. Often, this phenomenon is called "national mood". The national mood, John W. Kingdon noted, "changes from one time to another in discernable ways." He even goes further, arguing that "these changes in mood or climate have important impacts on policy agendas and policy outcomes."[103] However, whereas social scientists share the view that the aggregate of the American mind is generally quite stable and changes slowly in predictable ways, they differ on whether these opinion changes are important causes of policy change. It is the complexity of forces at work in a democracy; including the media, interest groups, political manipulation of the public agenda, etc., that makes it hard to achieve reliable research outcomes proving a linkage between policy and public opinion.[104]

---

[100] Ralph K. White, *Fearful Warriors – A Psychological Profile of U.S.-Soviet Relations*, New York, London, The Free Press, 1984, p. ix.

[101] Georgi Arbatov is former director of Moscow's Institute for U.S. and Canadian Studies; quoted in: Yale Richmond: *From Nyet to Da – Understanding the Russians*, Yarmouth, Intercultural Press, 1996, p. xv.

[102] For full names of the poll organizations abbreviated throughout the text, see Fig. 1 in the Appendix.

[103] quoted in: James A. Stimson, *Public Opinion in America*, Boulder, Westview Press, 1999, p. 1.

[104] Barbara A. Bardes, Robert W. Olderdick, *Public Opinion – Measuring the American Mind*, Toronto, Thomson & Wadsworth, 2003, pp. 244-245.

On the other hand, there is no doubt that outside factors have an influence on public opinion. Most of what Americans learned about the actions of the Soviet Union came from governmental leaders and the media. Brett Silverstein and Catherine Flamenbaum, in 1987, studied the effect of biases on how U.S. citizens processed information regarding the actions of the Soviet Union. They presupposed that "[a]n image of an enemy develops from incoming information: sometimes from perceptions of the enemy's actions or statements, but more frequently from perception of reports of the enemy's actions or statements." Several studies have demonstrated that people, when perceiving enemies, are likely to attend to, encode and remember threatening actions more readily than when perceiving non-enemies. Accusations against enemies will be more influential and more memorable than statements that deny enemy wrongdoing. Hence, Americans who read about the actions of the Soviet Union tended to recall the hostile actions. Their perceptions of the Soviets as hostile, Silverstein and Flamenbaum proved, were thereby strengthened, leading to an exaggerated enemy image.[105] In 1980, a Gallup poll found 73 percent of Americans had an unfavorable attitude toward the Soviet Union.[106]

How has the American perception of Russia changed since then? What kinds of trends occurred in American attitudes toward their former enemy? Stimson, in this respect, defines "trend" as a public opinion time series that appears to move systematically and by regular increments. He stresses the latter part of his definition because most of what is called a "trend" is in fact a drift, a series that moves substantially but not regularly.[107] The terms "trend" and "drift" will hereafter be used according to Stimson's definitions. It is important to note that there is a big difference between survey outcomes of "open" and "closed" questions. An open question affords the opportunity for a creative response, allowing the person to focus on relatively personal matters, such as the family financial situation or health. An example of an open question is "What do you worry about most?" Even when put in national terms such a question allows the person to give spontaneous answers within a wide range of possible personal priorities. Closed questions force the person to focus on just one particular issue with only a few possible answers like "yes", "no", or "don't know". Although closed question polls give information on how the population is thinking about a particular issue, they must be taken with a grain of salt because they often give a distorted picture of the issue's real importance in the respondents' lives.

---

[105] Brett Silverstein, Catherine Flamenbaum, Biases in the Perception and Cognition of the Actions of Enemies, in: *Journal of Social Issues* 45/ 2, 1989, pp. 51-54.
[106] reported in: Tom W. Smith, The Polls – American Attitudes Toward the Soviet Union and Communism, in: *Public Opinion Quarterly* 47, 1983, p. 280.
[107] Stimson, cited above, pp. 8-9.

6. The Perception of Soviet Military Strength and Nuclear Anxiety

Before analyzing the patterns in the perception of the Soviet Union or Russia as a threat and danger, it is important to look first on how, over the years, Americans evaluated the military power of the Soviet Union and the possibility of a nuclear war. After détente, Soviet-American relations chilled. This was caused in part by the huge Soviet arms buildup. A CBS/NYT poll (see Table 1 in the Appendix), conducted from 1981 until 1990, shows that there had never been a majority of Americans who thought that the U.S. was superior in military strength to the Soviet Union. In fact, those believing in U.S. superiority never exceeded 21 percent. Most years, the majority of Americans thought that both superpowers were about equal in military strength. Only in the period form 1981 to 1983 did a majority of Americans have feelings of military inferiority. It was the peak of a trend, which started in the late 1970s. Although after 1983 this majority ceased to exist, there remained a third of the American public who perceived the Soviets were ahead, compared to the much smaller percentage, who believed that it was vice versa.[108]

The United States, in the early 1980s, experienced a huge military buildup. The American defense budget grew by nearly 25 percent in real terms between 1980 and 1982. Ralph K. White concluded, "... if we assume a rough equality already in, say, 1980, the United States was jumping ahead in total defense expenditures at a rate the USSR, with only half its Gross Annual Product, could hardly be expected to match." This, according to White, demonstrates "how false the myth of Soviet nuclear superiority" was.[109]

For many years, the United States and the Soviet Union had possessed sufficient nuclear weapons to destroy much of human civilization, and perhaps the human race itself. At the beginning of the 1980s, in the face of such potential disaster, many, including scientists and political leaders, believed that the most serious problem facing the United States was the threat of nuclear war. However, although Americans viewed nuclear war as more likely than most nationalities did,[110] a strong concern about nuclear war had seldom been so pressing. Even when in 1982 a majority of Americans saw the Soviet Union as militarily superior, a Gallup poll found fewer than 10 percent of the American adult population mentioned the threat of war of any kind when asked: "What do you think is the most important problem facing the country today?" Other issues like inflation and unemployment always ranked higher. One of the reasons for such a ranking, Howard Shuman, Jacob Ludwig and John Krosnick suggested,

---

[108] reported in: Alvin Richman, Alvin, The Polls—Poll Trends; Changing American Attitudes Toward the Soviet Union, in: *Public Opinion Quarterly* 55, 1991, p. 142.

[109] White, cited above, p. 335.

[110] Tom W. Smith, The Polls – A Report; Nuclear Anxiety, in: Public *Opinion Quarterly* 52, 1988, p. 558.

was that the threat of nuclear war came to mind less easily since much of the time this issue was not in the news, nor was it connected directly to daily life.[111]

Nonetheless, between July and December 1983, the "threat of nuclear war" category rose by 17 percent, to approximately 24 percent of Americans thinking that it was the most important problem facing the United States. Two factors led to this sudden emergence of the perceived nuclear threat. First, the likelihood of war appears to have peaked in 1982-83 as further crises rocked the international scene, the peace movement surged in Europe and the nuclear freeze movement[112] gained ground in the United States. Second, as the findings of Shuman, Ludwig and Krosnick suggest, the general publicity of a film, *The Day After*, about the effects of such a war, had a tremendous impact on the public. The television showing of the film was one of the best publicized news events about nuclear war in the last months of 1983. Nuclear war and related issues in general were mentioned frequently in news reports in the beginning of 1982, then dropped to a lower level, but rose to their highest frequency at the end of 1983.[113] A poll conducted by the Public Agenda Foundation to probe attitudes toward nuclear arms for 1984 found, that by 89 percent to 9 percent, Americans subscribed to the view that "there can be no winner in an all-out nuclear war; both the United States and the Soviet Union would be completely destroyed."[114] Since then, however, the succession of Reagan-Gorbachev summits culminating in the INF treaty and a diminution of spot crises have led to a notable decline in the public's evaluation of the probability of nuclear war.[115]

---

[111] Howard Schuman, Jacob Ludwig, Jon A. Krosnick, The Perceived Threat of Nuclear War, Salience, and Open Questions, in: *Public Opinion Quarterly* 50, 1986, pp. 520-521.

[112] For a detailed discussion of public support of the nuclear freeze movement, see J. Michael Hogan, Ted J. Smith III, Polling on the Issues – Public Opinion and the Nuclear Freeze, in: *Public Opinion Quarterly* 55, 1991, pp. 534-569.

[113] Howard Shuman, Jacob Ludwig, John A. Krosnick: The Perceived Threat of Nuclear War, Salience and Open Questions, in: *Public Opinion Quarterly* 50, 1986, pp. 528-530.

[114] reported in: Daniel Yankelovich, John Doble, The Public Mood: Nuclear Weapons and the U.S.S.R., in: *Foreign Affairs* 63/1, 1984, pp. 33-34.

[115] Smith (1988), cited above, p. 559.

7. The Declining Perception of the Soviet Union/Russia as a Threat

Mainly, three factors had an impact on the American perception of the Soviet Union as a threat: its military strength, its struggle for world dominance, and the ideological commitment to spread communism throughout the world. The decline in the evaluation of the probability of nuclear war in the late 1980s makes the declining perception cf the Soviet Union as a military threat easier to comprehend (despite the fact, that constantly until the end of the 1980s, almost a third of Americans saw the Soviet Union as militarily superior). A CBS/NYT poll conducted throughout the 1980s asked: "Do you believe the military threat from the Soviet Union is constantly growing and presents a real, immediate danger to the United States, or not?" From the most pessimistic outcome at the end of 1983, when 64 percent of the respondents answered "yes", the percentage fell to 54 percent in 1985 (which was not a great difference to the 57 percent of early 1983).

Thereafter, however, within a mere four years, the figure fell to 26 percent in 1989, with a large majority (65%) thinking that the military threat from the Soviet Union is not growing and that there is no real, immediate danger to the United States. Another CBS/NYT question read, "Generally, would you describe the Soviet Union as a peace-loving nation willing to fight only if it thinks it has to defend itself, or as an aggressive nation that would start a war to get something it wants." In 1985, a large majority (69%) of Americans took the view that the Soviet Union was aggressive. Throughout the following five years, this perception changed profoundly. In 1990, just 38 percent viewed it as aggressive while 43 percent viewed it as peace-loving (compared to the 17 percent of 1985).[116]

This trend of a sharp decline in the perception of the Soviet Union as a military threat in the late 1980s is reflected in a similar trend in American public opinion on dealing with the adversary on the level of foreign affairs. In 1980, Roper found that only 16 percent of Americans agreed with the statement, "We should do nothing that is likely to provoke a U.S.-Russian military conflict, but instead try to negotiate and reason out our differences." According to a Harris poll from 1981, more than 70 percent of Americans agreed with the following: "By sending military aid to countries threatened by communism and being tough with the Russians, Reagan will rebuild respect for the U.S. in the Kremlin." However, polls conducted by CBS/NYT and ATS show that public attitude toward a "get-tough" posture changed sharply within the following years of the Reagan era. Whereas in 1980 only 20 percent agreed with the statement, "The U.S. should try harder to reduce tension with the Russians versus getting tougher

---

[116] reported in: Richman, cited above, pp. 141-142.

in its dealings with them", the figure rose to 42 percent in 1985 and 64 percent in 1987.[117]

The Chicago Council on Foreign Relations (CCFR), from 1990-2002, conducted a survey on the possible threat of Russia's military power to the vital interests of the United States. Throughout the whole decade, a large majority (49%-57%) of the respondents saw it as important but not a critical threat. The percentage of those who viewed it as a critical threat remained almost constant from 1990 until 1998, with a slight drift up to 34 percent in 1998 due to friction between the U.S. and Russia over Iraq. However, this figure declined sharply during the next four years to 23 percent in 2002.[118]

But, to what extent did ideology play a role in the changing American attitude toward the Soviet Union or Russia? As various survey data suggest, the attitudes of the American public toward the Soviet Union and communism as a social system are highly complex. Social scientists found that the label "communist" arouses a diffuse negative affect in most Americans.[119] Interestingly, a national Gallup survey found that the external threat from communism was not particularly salient for most Americans. When asked an open question about their personal hopes and fears regarding the future of the United States, "threat of communism or aggression by communist power" showed a steady decline from 29 percent in 1964, to 13 percent in 1974, to a low 8 percent in March 1981, a time when the new Reagan Administration practiced a strong anticommunist rhetoric. The public, in 1981, had turned to other concerns, most of all the U.S. economy.[120] Yancelovich and John Doble, in 1984, found another reason why there was little fear of communist subversion in the United States:

> Today, the majority of Americans have reached a conclusion about communism that can best be described as pragmatic rejection. As they have in the past, Americans today firmly reject the social values of communism, and see them opposed to all our fundamental beliefs. But there is little fear today that communist subversion threatens the United States, that communists will engage in sabotage, form a fifth column, or convert millions of Americans to their cause.[121]

---

[117] reported in: Daniel Yankelovich, Richard Smoke, America's „New Thinking," in: *Foreign Affairs* 67/1, 1988, pp. 4-5.

[118] CCFR (Chicago Council on Foreign Relations): "Worldviews 2002 Survey of American and European Attitudes," Chapter 6; Internet Site: <http://www.worldviews.org/ detailreports/usreport /html/ch6s3. html> (accessed 14 November 2003).

[119] Smith, cited above, p. 291.

[120] Choichiro Yatani, Dana Bramel, Trends and Patterns in American's Attitudes Toward the Soviet Union, in: *Journal of Social Issues* 45/2, 1989, p. 19.

[121] Daniel Yankelovich, John Doble, The Public Mood: Nuclear Weapons and the U.S.S.R., in: *Foreign Affairs* 63/1, 1984, pp. 33-46., pp. 38-39.

In 1984, the Public Agenda Foundation asked a series of questions on why the Soviet Union might be considered an enemy of the United States. The argument that "they try to spread communist revolution to other countries" was judged as very important by 69% of the sample. However, the addition of the term "communist" to the implied rivalry in the statement did not push agreement much higher than with other expansionism items.[122] Roper polls have shown a peak in the percentage (73%) who perceived "global domination" as the USSR's main foreign-policy objective in 1980. It then appears most Americans put global power rivalry above anticommunism as the main perceived determinant of an anti-Soviet orientation. Throughout the 1980s, however, Roper found a steady decline of the percentage viewing the Soviet Union as eager to achieve global domination to 58 percent in late 1984, shortly before Gorbachev's accession to power, and 25 percent in early 1990 (see Fig. 1)[123]

To sum up, it is not important whether the majority felt personally more or less threatened by the ideological or by the power rivalry aspect. Of prime importance is that the USSR's official intention to spread communism throughout the world led to an assertive anticommunist, anti-Soviet mood in the early Reagan years, when Americans were ready to support cold-war kinds of initiatives. When the same respondents of the Public Agenda Foundation survey from 1984 had to choose between whether they worry more about the "military threat to the United States," or the "threat to all our beliefs and values – freedom, democracy, religion, and free enterprise," only 26 percent chose the first alternative, while 69 percent chose the second.[124] Hence, there is no doubt that the end of communist rule in the former Soviet Union at the beginning of the 1990s must have had a profound impact on the changing American attitude toward Russia. When in 1989 Harris asked respondents, whether they agree or disagree with the statement: "As long as the communists are in control in Moscow, it will be almost impossible to find ways to ease the world's fear of nuclear war", a majority (about 55%) agreed.[125] Americans, however, were aware that the Soviet Union was undergoing change. According to a Harris poll, conducted in 1988, about 42 percent of Americans thought that the communist system in the Soviet Union was undergoing "minor changes," about 35 percent that it was undergoing "major changes", and only about 18 percent felt that there was "not much change at all."[126] An Associated Press poll by November 1989

---

[122] Yatani, Bramel, cited above, p. 24.

[123] reported in: Richman, cited above, p. 136.

[124] Yatani, Bramel, cited above, p. 24.

[125] Source: Harris (Louis Harris and Associates), Date: 9/1989; Internet Site: <http://www.irss. unc.edu/ data_archive/pollsearch.html> (accessed 14 November 2003).

[126] Source: Harris, Date: 07/1988; Internet Site: <http://www.irss.unc.edu/ data_archive/ pollsearch.html> (accessed 4 November 2003).

found that 54 percent of Americans believed that communism around the world was on the decline.[127]

How sharply the public's perception of the Soviet Union as a threat in general declined in the late 1980s is demonstrated by an ATS poll, which in 1988 found 57 percent of Americans believing that the Soviet Union was a serious threat to the United States. By 1990, this figure sank to 33 percent, while the majority (49%) viewed it a minor threat and 16 percent (compared to only 8 percent in 1988) as not being a threat at all. In 1996, when a PIPA survey offered two statements about the nature of Russia, 66 percent opted for the one that said, "Russia is not necessarily aggressive by nature. If democracy succeeds there, it is likely that Russia will behave peacefully toward the West." Only 30 percent embraced the argument that Russia is aggressive by nature. It will just be a matter of time before Russia regains its strength and tries to use its military aggressively. A few years later, a Time/CNN poll found that whereas in 2000 still only 18 percent of Americans believed Russia not to be a threat at all, this figure rose to 41 percent in 2002. This sharp increase in optimistic perception, undoubtedly, was a consequence of the renewed U.S-Russian relationship after the terrorist attacks of September 11, 2001.

Although Americans are not concerned about the Russian threat presently, this does not mean they completely discount the idea of Russia again becoming a threat in the future. When a May 2002 Fox News poll asked, "Do you think the Cold War is really over, or will Russia be an enemy of the U.S. again?" About 36 percent said the Cold War was over, while 40 percent felt that Russia would be an enemy again. This is consistent with polls from 1996 and 1998, when PIPA asked respondents to rate, on a scale of 0 to 10, the likelihood that Russia will become a threat sometime in the future. Whereas in 1996 the mean response was 4.89 it rose to 5.51 in 1998 due to friction between the U.S. and Russia over Iraq. This tendency of volatile responses, which seem to be very dependent on the particular news of the day, implies that Russia, for most Americans, still does not appear to be a stable and absolute trustworthy nation. A CCFR survey, conducted in 2002, supports this conclusion. According to the survey, Americans view Russian domestic problems as a threat to the U.S. on the same level as Russian military power. When respondents were asked to rate the level of threat to the United States of "political turmoil in Russia," 27 percent felt it to be a critical threat, 58 percent categorized it as important, but not critical, and just 13 percent felt that political turmoil in Russia was not an important threat.[128]

---

[127] reported in: Bardes, cited above, p. 240.
[128] reported in: PIPA, "Americans and the World" (Public Opinion on International Affairs); Report: Americans on Russia (last revised November 22, 2002); Internet site: <http://www.americans-world.org/digest/regional_issues/ russia/summary.cfm> (accessed 10 September 2003).

8. Trends in the General Attitudes toward the Soviet Union/Russia

The same reasons for the trend in the declining perception of the Soviet Union/Russia as a threat have caused a decline in American hostility toward their former adversary. National survey questions with repeated use of standard global favorability questions about the Soviet Union have been asked by NORC/GSS since 1974. The respondents were asked to rate for the Soviet Union on as scale of "minus 5" to "plus 5." These data show that Americans expressed rising negativity toward the Soviets from 1974 until 1983, then declining hostility until 1990 (see Fig. 1: "Negative Scalometer Ratings of Russia"). Accordingly, the poll found that whereas in the early 1980s only about one fifth of Americans expressed a favorable opinion of the Soviet Union, the improvement of the overall image throughout the decade led to three fifths of Americans having a favorable opinion by 1990.[129]

Fig. 1

Changing American Attitudes toward the Soviet Union

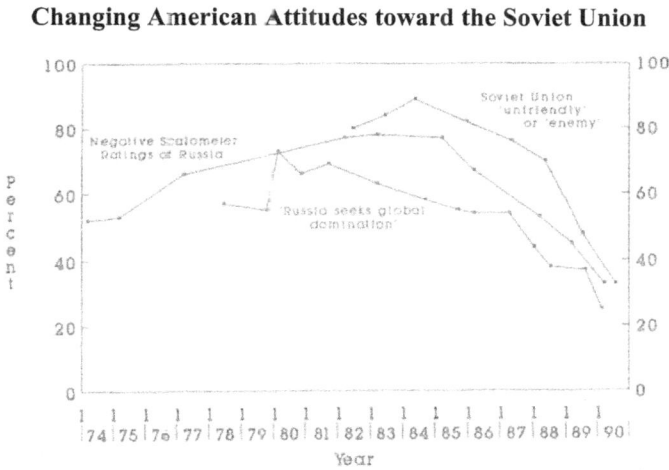

Source: Richman, Alvin (1991): The Polls-Poll Trends: Changing American Attitudes toward the Soviet Union, in: Public Opinion Quarterly 55: 137.

Another survey, conducted by Roper since 1982, has regularly asked respondents to rate the Soviet Union on a five-point scale ranging from "close ally" to "enemy" of the United States. The ratings hit bottom in 1984, with 49 percent terming it an "enemy" and another 40 percent "unfriendly." Since then, according to the survey, negative views of Soviet policies had dropped sharply until the end of the decade. In 1990, just 10 percent of the respondents rated the

---

[129] reported in: Richman, cited above, p 145.

Soviet Union as "enemy" and 23 percent as "unfriendly" (see Fig. 1: "Soviet Union 'unfriendly' or 'enemy'). This decline among those viewing the Soviet Union negatively is matched by a rise in the percentage viewing it either as "neutral" toward the United States (up from 4 percent in 1984 to 31 percent in 1990) or as "friendly" to the United States (up from 2 percent to 20 percent).[130]

Notwithstanding this trend of optimism Yankelovich and Smoke, in 1988, observed that although there was a striking pattern of change in the public attitude, it was likewise ambivalent:

> The current attitude of Americans toward the Soviet Union is different from anything we have seen in forty years. It is not the troubled mood of recent years, of worry about nuclear war. It is not the mood of the beginning of this decade, when Americans assertively endorsed a strong military buildup. It is not the mood of the early 1970s, when Americans were overly optimistic about the possibilities of détente. Nor is it the cold war mood of the 1950s and early 1960s. The majority of Americans are now interested in neither a further military buildup nor instant friendship. The current mood can be characterized as a wary readiness. It is a readiness of a special kind: distinctly hopeful yet cautious….The country remains suspicious and mistrustful of the Soviets.[131]

Harris, in August 1989, asked respondents to agree or disagree with the statement: "Even though [Gorbachev] looks more modern and attractive, it would be a mistake to think he is really much different from other Russian leaders." A majority of about 51 percent agreed, while about 46 percent disagreed.[132] A few months later, a Time-CNN/Yankelovich poll found 78 percent preferred that President Bush "remain cautious in his dealings with the Soviets," rather than "act quickly to take advantage of recent changes in the Soviet Union" (16%).[133]

This cautious American attitude toward the USSR shortly before it dissolved, together with the cooling relationship between the two countries on a government-to-government level during the 1990s, seem to be the main reasons for a seven-year cooling trend in the public's general perception of Russia from 1993 to 2000. Harris, throughout the whole period, asked respondents to decide whether they "feel that Russia is a close ally of the U.S., is friendly, but not a close ally, is not friendly, but not an enemy, or is unfriendly and is an enemy of the U.S." As the following graphic (see Fig. 2) shows, the percentage of

---

[130] Ibid., pp. 137-138.
[131] Yankelovich, Smoke, cited above, pp. 1-2.
[132] Source: Harris, Date: 08/89, Internet site: : <http://www.irss.unc.edu/ data_archive/pollsearch. html> (accessed 14 November 2003).
[133] reported in: Richman, cited above, p. 139.

Americans thinking that Russia is friendly or a close ally declined steadily from 66 percent in 1993 down to 36 percent in 2000 (see Table 2 in the Appendix)[134]

Fig. 2

Do you feel that Russia ... is a close ally of the US (United States), is friendly but not a close ally, is not friendly but not an enemy, or is unfriendly and is an enemy of the US?

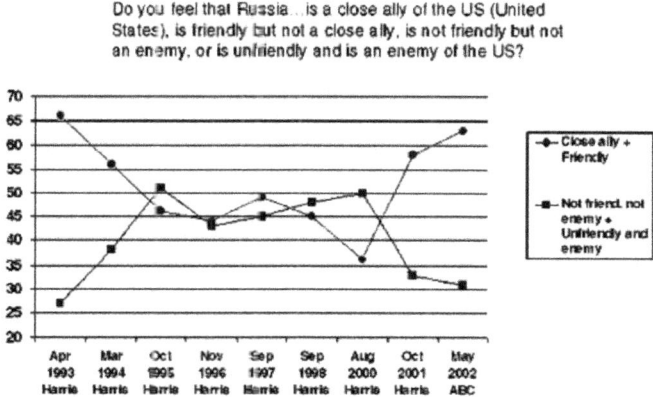

Source: PIPA, Internet site: ' Americans and the World" (Public Opinion on International Affairs): Americans on Russia (last revised November 22, 2002); Internet site: <www.americans-world.org/digest/regional_issues/russia/summary.cfm>.

The graphic in Fig. 2 also shows that the cooling trend has sharply reversed since the beginning of 2001, replaced by a warming trend in attitudes toward Russia. Although this trend was already in place before September 11, it appears that it may have further consolidated in response to Russian cooperation in the war on terrorism. The CCFR in its Worldviews 2002 Report summarized the reasons for the changed American view on U.S. foreign politics and Russia after this shock:

> The terrorist attacks of 9/11 and their aftermath have significantly altered how Americans view key countries and U.S. relationships with them around the globe. The new sense of vulnerability and the imperative of countering terrorism have heightened the importance of old friends and allies, altered the perception of foes and threats, and raised the awareness of new players and risks. One marked response is a "huddling impulse," a greater priority attached to long-time, reliable

---

[134] reported in: PIPA website "Americans and the World" (Public Opinion on International Affairs); Report: Americans on Russia (last revised November 22, 2002); Internet site: <www.americans-world.org/digest/regional_issues/ russia/summary.cfm> (accessed 10 September 2003).

partners, especially U.S. allies in Europe and Canada. A very notable addition to the 'huddle' is Russia.[135]

In April 2002, Hart and Teeter Research Companies/NBC News/Wall Street Journal conducted a poll, asking respondents whether they in general "think of Russia as more an ally or more an adversary." A majority of 52 percent said that they thought of Russia as more of an ally. Only 26 percent chose the "more of an adversary" option. The rest of the respondents refused to make a concrete choice.[136]

The degree to which Russia has been transformed from enemy to partner is perhaps most striking in the 68 percent of Americans who, according to the CCFR poll in 2002, favored the expansion of NATO to include Russia.[137] This attitude is especially noteworthy because it appears little more than 10 years after the end of the Cold War, when NATO was dedicated to defense against the Soviet Union. The recent growth in willingness to see Russia eventually join NATO was foreshadowed in earlier PIPA results. In 1996 and 1998, PIPA questioned respondents about their attitudes toward Russia within the context of NATO enlargement. In both polls, of all the reasons not to enlarge NATO to the east, the most popular was that such a policy was not inclusive enough. It read, "Instead of expanding NATO, something new should be developed that includes Russia rather than treating Russia as an enemy."[138]

---

[135] Source: CCFR (Chicago Council on Foreign Relations): "Worldviews 2002", Chapter 6; Internet Site: <http://www.worldviews.org/ detailreports/usreport/html/ch6s3.html> (accessed 14 November 2003).

[136] reported in: PIPA website "Americans and the World" (Public Opinion on International Affairs); Report: Americans on Russia (last revised November 22, 2002); Internet site: <www.americans-world.org/digest/regional_issues/ russia/summary.cfm> (accessed 10 September 2003).

[137] Source: CCFR (Chicago Council on Foreign Relations): "Worldviews 2002", Chapter 3; Internet Site: <http://www.worldviews.org/ detailreports/ usreport/html/ch3s9.html> (accessed 14 November 2003).

[138] reported in: PIPA website "Americans and the World" (Public Opinion on International Affairs); Report: Americans on Russia (last revised November 22, 2002); Internet site: <www.americans-world.org/digest/regional_issues/ russia/summary.cfm> (accessed 10 September 2003).

9. The Current Perception of Russia in the United States

A major reason for the increased preference for an inclusive approach with regard to Russia is the interest Americans have in seeing Russia stable. When PIPA, in its 1998 poll offered two statements, only 30 percent embraced the position that "There are too many ways that our interests might come into conflict with Russia in the future and there is always the chance that Russia may go back to being aggressive. Therefore, it is not a good idea to include Russia in NATO." A large majority of 64 percent, however, chose the one that said, "Once Russia has shown that it can be stable and peaceful for a significant period we should try to include it in NATO. This will help assure that Russia will stay stable and peaceful." A Gallup poll in 2000 asked respondents to estimate how important events in Russia are to the United States. The majority (46%) thought it to be "vitally important," 40 percent "important, but not vital," 8 percent "not too important", and only 3 percent thought it to be "not at all important."[139]

The June 2002 CCFR survey asked respondents to rate the influence of listed countries in the world on a scale of 0-10. The mean response for Russia was 6.5, which placed it fifth after the U.S. (9.1), Great Britain (7.0), China (6.8), European Union (6.7). Many traditional allies, such as Germany and France were individually ranked lower. The same survey found that a majority of Americans (55%) thought that, in world affairs, Russia would play a "greater role…in the next ten years" while only 35 percent felt that it would play a "lesser role." This represents a solid boost for those arguing Russia will play a greater role: in 1998 and 1994, the public had been evenly divided (44% to 44%) as to whether Russia would play a greater or lesser role in the future.[140]

Americans, for a number of reasons, concluded that the U.S. has a vital interest in Russia for security reasons. The instability of Russia itself, its possession of nuclear weapons, its influence on unstable regions surrounding it, the expected future influence of Russia in world affairs, and its willingness to support the U.S. in the war on terrorism were all contributing factors. There are other reasons as well that make Russia important to the United States, mainly its right of veto in the United Nations Security Council and its energy resources. Throughout the last decade, large majorities of Americans have consistently viewed Russia as a vital interest for the U.S. A 2002 CCFR poll, for example,

---

[139] reported in: PIPA, "Americans and the World" (Public Opinion on International Affairs); Report: Americans on Russia (last revised November 22, 2002); Internet site: <www.americans-world.org/digest/regional_issues/ russia/summary.cfm> (accessed 12 September 2003).
[140] Source: CCFR (Chicago Council on Foreign Relations): "Worldviews 2002", Chapter 6; Internet Site: <http://www.worldviews.org/ detailreports/usreport/html/ch6s3.html> (accessed 14 November 2003).

found an astonishing 81 percent of Americans thinking Russia to be a vital interest of the United States.[141]

Of great importance to Americans in their relation to Russia today seems to be the partnership in the war on terrorism. In the June 2002 poll by CCFR, almost 3 in 4 (74%) saw Russia as a "reliable partner" in the U.S. war on terrorism. Just 19 percent felt that it was not a reliable partner. It is interesting to note that although Russia, in early 2003, used its United Nations veto against U.S. intervention in Iraq, the trend of the warming attitude toward Russia has not altered. The August 2002 Harris poll found about 14 percent of Americans thought of Russia as a "close ally." This percentage even increased by 1 percent in August 2003. The percentage that saw Russia as "friendly, but not a close ally" decreased by only 1 percent (from 44% to 43%). The share of Americans who had a neutral attitude toward Russia ("not friendly, not enemy") fell from 35 percent in 2002 to 32 percent in 2003. The percentage of those perceiving Russia as "unfriendly and enemy" increased from 8 to 10 percent. Altogether, neither the percentage of those with a favorable perception of Russia ("close ally" + "friendly, but not close ally") nor the percentage of those having a neutral or unfavorable opinion ("not friendly, not enemy" + "unfriendly and enemy") had changed between August 2002 and August 2003 (for a better overview see Table 3 in the Appendix).[142] Despite disagreement between the U.S. and Russia regarding such an important issue as Iraq, Americans positive attitude toward Russia did not decrease. The Americans' relationship to and perception of Russia, it appears, are strong and stable enough to overcome future inconsistencies of great significance.

On the other hand, Americans do not seem to feel very convinced about the future partnership with Russia. They have not completely discounted the idea of Russia again becoming a threat in the future. Although Russia's United Nations veto against the U.S. invasion of Iraq, in early 2003, does not seem to have had an effect on the generally positive American attitude toward the Russians, it left many Americans with a great uncertainty of whether Russia is a real strategic partner of the United States. The CCFR thermometer ratings of general feelings toward Russia clearly reflect this rather ambivalent perception of Russia. According to a survey in 2002, general feelings among Americans nowadays are higher than in 1998 (49°) and well above the levels found during

---

[141] reported in: PIPA, "Americans and the World" (Public Opinion on International Affairs); Report: Americans on Russia (last revised November 22, 2002); Internet site: <www.americans-world.org/digest/regional_issues/ russia/summary.cfm> (accessed 12 September 2003).
[142] Ibid.

the Cold War era (ranging between 26° and 34°), they are still only moderately warm (55°).[143]

Moreover, Russia is still far from being a close ally, that is, someone who helps and supports the U.S. in difficult situations, especially in a war. Accordingly, throughout the nineties, the percentage of Americans who viewed Russia as a "close ally" never exceeded 10 percent (see Table 2 in the Appendix). This percentage suddenly rose to 17 percent in October 2001, shortly after Russia had expressed its solidarity with the United States in the fight against terrorism. Although the amount of Americans, who think Russia to be a "close ally" is higher today than in the decade before, it still does not exceed 15 percent (see Table 3 in the Appendix). However, the fact that a majority of Americans wants to see Russia join NATO clearly shows that most Americans wish for the Russians to be their future allies.

---

[143] Source: CCFR (Chicago Council on Foreign Relations): "Worldviews 2002", Chapter 6; Internet Site: <http://www.wcrldviews.org/ detailreports/usreport/html/ch6s3.html> (accessed 14 November 2003).

III CROSS-CULTURAL CONTACT

10. Cross-Cultural Communication

> *Misunderstandings do not exist, only
> the failure to communicate.*
>
> -- South-East Asian proverb

To overcome discrepancies, fears, anger, suspicions or prejudices in the relationship between two individuals, communication is imperative. The same applies to the relationship between two nations because nations, after all, consist of individuals. Only through fruitful communication, can enemies become friends. It is only natural that a great number of the respondents of the "Friends and Enemies" project defined a national friend as a country with which Americans have "good communications." Cross-cultural communication in the general sense is defined as the direct or indirect exchange of information between representatives of different linguistic cultures.[144] Every nation has its own culture, with a history, a language and customs its people share. The communication between representatives of two different cultures is more difficult than the communication between representatives of the same culture because cultural differences constitute communication barriers, which have to be overcome to achieve mutual understanding.

A traditional subject in the field of cross-cultural research is the comparison of high-contextual and low-contextual cultures. Cultures are low-contextual when the major part of the information in a conversation is encoded on an explicit level. In high-contextual cultures, on the contrary, a large part of the information is encoded on the level of (internal and/or external) context. Features of high-contextual cultures appear to be their strong tradition, stability, emotionality, and their aversion to change, while low-contextual cultures are associated with dynamism and a high standard of technological development. Practically, all researchers without hesitation classify the American culture as a low-contextual culture. The Russian culture, however, cannot be categorized that easily. Russia, throughout its long history experienced important influences from the West as well as from the East, and therefore occupies a place between low-contextual (western) and high-contextual (eastern) cultures.

On the one-hand side, Russians are proud of their directness and express the information explicitly enough (for example, in business-like situations); on the other side, in the emotional sphere, they tend to encode parts of the information in an implicit, indirect, more complicated form. When

---

[144] Leontovitsh, cited above, pp. 6-7.

representatives of different cultures meet, there is a danger of both underestimation and overestimation of the role of context in a conversation. Americans, for example, often do not fully take into account the role of contextual information in their conversations with representatives of high-contextual cultures. This results in their partner's perception of American behavior as impolite and tactless. Americans, on the other hand, often blame representatives of high-contextual cultures for their unwillingness to express their thoughts honestly and clearly. In general, cross-cultural communication is characterized by an exchange of rather low-contextual information, since the participants are usually intuitively aware of their foreign partners not being familiar enough with the different cultural context.[145]

Nonetheless, to achieve a high level of mutual understanding, communicators from different cultures, most of all, must understand the cultural codes of their partner. There are two different types of codes: The internal code ("the language of the thoughts") contains all personal experiences a person remembers and uses as a basis to absorb new information. The external code embraces first, a person's general way of expressing herself or himself verbally (most of all by using a specific language), and second, non-verbal signals, such as gestures, facial expression or mime.[146] The more common elements the communicators share, the higher the possibility of mutual understanding. Perhaps, the main feature Americans and Russians share is to "think big," as Yale Richmond expressed it.[147] Both nations have in common the huge territorial expanses and the variety of natural conditions. The historical parallels, like the expansion to the West by the Americans and the opening up of Siberia by the Russians, as well as the feeling to be a part of a vast nation condition the self-identification of Russians and Americans and their relation with representatives of other cultures. It appears, however, that the cultural differences between Americans and Russians by far outweigh the cultural similarities.

---

[145] Leontovitsh, cited above, pp. 52-53.

[146] B.S. Erasov, *Sotsial'naic kul'torologija*, Moscow, Aspect Press, 1997, p. 445.

[147] Richmond, cited above, p. xxi.

11. Stereotypes versus Real Differences

*Familiarization with the differences
is the first step to bridging them.*

-- Yale Richmond[148]

Because of the uniqueness of their geographical location, their comparability with regard to the territorial dimensions and their influence in the world, the Soviet Union and the United States in the course of several decades opposed each other on the global arena. Under these circumstances both sides also competed on the cross-cultural level. Americans and Russians developed the habit of examining each other and comparing their own situation with that of the rival. Because there were almost no possibilities to really get to know each other, due to almost no personal contacts, stereotypes in the perception of the opposite became the rule. The term *stereotype*, in Allport's words, means a "picture in our heads" that "simplifies complex social reality to manageable, if false, proportions."[149]

Urie Bronfenbrenner, in 1961, noted that the Soviets' distorted view of Americans was curiously similar to the American distorted picture of the Soviets.[150] Gallup, in 1942, asked respondents to choose adjectives descriptive of "Russians," and found that the top five rank order were *hardworking, brave, radical, ordinary,* and *progressive*. But a 1948 UNESCO poll done in the United States showed that *cruel* had moved to the top. In 1966, the last year this question was used, Gallup's top five adjectives to describe "Russians" were *hardworking, warlike, intelligent, progressive,* and *treacherous*.[151] The respondents of the "Friends and Enemies" project in 1985/86 mentioned *hardworking, patriotic, decent, suspicious,* and *aggressive* as the most frequent descriptors for the Russian people.[152]

Americans had an exaggerated negative image of the Soviet government's behavior. Shawn M. Burn and Stuart Oskamp, in 1989, while trying to measure the content of Americans' stereotypes in this respect, found from a questionnaire of American community college adults that most of the respondents interpreted Soviet actions more harshly than the very same actions when ascribed to the United States.[153] R. K. White, in 1985, was convinced that world peace would

---

[148] quoted in: Leontovitsh, cited above, pp. 104-105.

[149] quoted in: Holt, cited above, p. 36.

[150] Urie Bronfenbrenner, The mirror image in Soviet-American relations, in: *Journal of Social Issues,* 17/3, 1961, pp. 45-56.

[151] reported in: Choichiro, Bramel, cited above, p. 14.

[152] Holt, cited above, p. 46.

[153] Shawn M. Burn, Stuart Oskamp, Ingroup Biases and the U.S.-Soviet Conflict, in: *Journal of Social Issues* 45/2, 1989, p. 79.

be greatly enhanced by a greater humanization and knowledge of the other side. He wrote,

> Realistic empathy, not glossing over the evils of the Soviet system but getting rid of the monster image that now prevails the West, is greatly needed. In other words, we need to consider the situational as well as dispositional interpretations of the behavior of the actor, in this case the USSR.[154]

If Americans would have known more about the Soviets, then perhaps they would have stereotyped them less. In order to achieve real knowledge about the Russians, Americans, first of all, have to familiarize with the real differences between their own and the Russian culture. Most obviously, both nations have had different historical experiences. Whereas Americans in their comparably short history most of the time have experienced political and economic power and the leadership in the community of nations, "Russian and Soviet history is a much longer story of backwardness and isolation," as Robert English and Jonathan J. Harperlin noted in 1987. While analyzing the mutual perception of Soviets and Americans, English and Harperlin argued:

> Accepting the historical differences between our two societies and cultures is essential to understanding the perceptions that now dominate U.S. and Soviet thinking. We must appreciate the images of the past before we can fully comprehend our current dilemma.[155]

The differences in the psychological self-identification of Russians and Americans and their mutual perceptions in the process of cross-cultural communication is one of the most important reasons for the lack of understanding. It is impossible to give absolutely reliable and detailed definitions of the psychological identities of Americans and Russians. Nonetheless, both American and Russian researchers have made serious attempts to compare both identities. O.A. Leontovitsh summarized the results of these observations and listed seven types of differentiation:

1) *individualism* (Americans) versus *collectivism* (Russians)
2) *activism* (Americans) versus *passivism* (Russians)
3) *rationalism* (Americans) versus *emotionalism* (Russians)
4) *spirit of competition* (Americans) versus *spirit of cooperation* (Russians)
5) *optimism* (Americans) versus *pessimism* (Russians)
6) *tolerance (*Americans); *patience* (Russians)

---

[154] quoted in: Ibid., p. 74.
[155] Robert D. English, Jonathan J. Halperin, *The Other Side – How Soviets and Americans Perceive Each Other*, New Brunswick (U.S.A.), Oxford (U.K.), Transaction Books, 1987, p. 16.

7) *degree of openness*: higher with regard to *own opinion* and lower with regard to feelings/emotions (Americans) versus higher with regard to *feelings/emotions* and lower with regard to own opinion (Russians)

These simplified characterizations are not meant to define the psychological identity of every single individual of both cultures. The distinctions rather refer to both peoples as a whole. They were made by taking into account the different cultural-historical experiences of both societies, and therefore contain a considerable share of truth.[156]

---

[156] For the detailed discussion of the comparative analysis of the Russian and the American psychological identities see: Leontovitsh, cited above, pp. 210-232.

12. Knowledge – The Basis for Mutual Understanding

> *Understanding the Russians…remains a challenge for Americans*
> *for whom many aspects of Russian behavior may appear alien,*
> *but it is a challenge that must be met.*

-- Yale Richmond (1996)[157]

It is unrealistic to think that one can see all the wealth of a strange culture. It is possible, however, to develop knowledge about the peculiarities of a different culture and, therefore, to be able to decode the coded information in a conversation. But, to what extent could and did Americans develop the ability to perceive the signals of the Russian cultural code? Most of what the average American learns about current events in foreign countries, and about other cultures in general, comes from the media. By the average American, I refer to an American who is not a so-called "Russophile" with above-average interest in Russian culture, acting on his own to find the adequate amount of information on Russia in books, on the internet, or by studying Russian language or Russian history at the university. The so-called post-soviet scholars (earlier known as sovietologists) constitute the part of the American society that seriously and scientifically tries to decode the Russian cultural code, to "discover" Russia for Americans. Their books fill American libraries and contain information on Russia through an American perspective. It is from this material that not only Americans today, but also future generations can draw upon to better understand Russia and the Russians

Russia Coverage in the American Mass Media

Because the scope and the main purpose of this thesis do not allow a thorough media content analyses, the following study focuses on the quantity rather than the quality of Soviet Union/Russia coverage in the United States since 1980. With the help of the Lexis-Nexis database and the Vanderbilt News Archive, it was possible to examine how the quantity of USSR/Russia coverage has changed over the years in the *New York Times* and in the evening news of the major American TV news channels.[158]

---

[157] Richmond, cited above, p. xv.

[158] The method I used throughout the search in the Vanderbilt News Archive database is as follows: For the period from 1980 to 1990, I decided to search only for the term "USSR", after I made sure that the term "Soviet Union" brought no results and the results with the term "Russia" only (that is without "USSR"), were negligible for the general outcome. For 1991 and 1992, I used the terms "USSR" and "Russia" separately because the number of news items that contained the word "Russia" only was considerably high, and hence had an impact on the general result. For the period from 1993 to 2002, I searched only for the term "Russia" because results for the term

The graph in Fig. 3 (for exact figures see Table 4 in the Appendix) shows that in 1980 and 1981, when the tensions between the U.S. and the Soviet Union had heightened and sharp Cold War-like rhetoric was on the agenda, the evening news broadcasts on the major American TV news channels (ABC, CBS, NBC, CNN, CBS, and Fox) were filled with news mentioning the USSR. The highest occurrence of news items was reached in 1981 with 1279. Whereas USSR coverage declined in 1982, the number rose again until 1986 (1305), when it even topped the number of news items of 1981. Certainly, this increased attention Russia received in the evening news resulted from the appearance of Gorbachev in the limelight and the first rapprochement signals between him and President Reagan. The number of USSR-related news stories remained very high until the end of the 1980s. It reached another peak in 1990, the year when Gorbachev was faced with more and more problems that questioned his future existence as the leader of the Soviet Union. The 1352 news stories broadcasted throughout the whole year, represented the highest amount of evening news coverage dealing with the USSR/Russia ever.

"USSR" were negligible. I chose the option "all networks," which guaranteed the search for all evening news regarding the USSR in the databases of ABC, CBS, NBC, CNN, PBS, and Fox. (I chose this option because it provides for an average result with regard to the most influential TV news channels in the United States). Furthermore, I included results from "regular evening news broadcasts" and "news contents." Since the Chechen conflict had been one of the major issues in the evening news broadcasts regarding Russia since 1995, I used the term "Chechnya" together with the term "Russia" to filter those of the Russia related articles that mainly referred to this issue.

Fig. 3

USSR/Russia coverage in the evening news of ABC, CBS, NBC, CNN, PBS, Fox

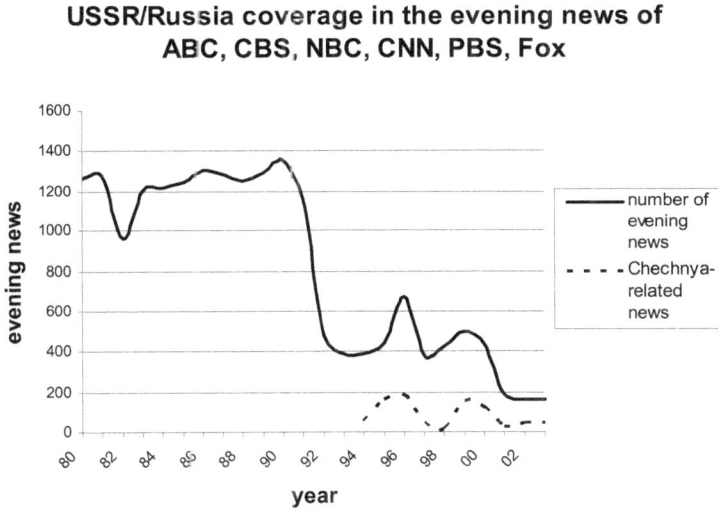

Source: Vanderbilt News Archive; Internet site: <http://tvnews.vanderbilt.edu>.

From the moment, the Soviet Union dissolved and the Cold War was over, the number of news items dealing with Russia decreased by an astonishing 65 percent in just two years (1991-1992) with only 474 evening news broadcast throughout 1992 on all major U.S. news networks. Despite two exceptions in 1996 and 1998, the curve shows a further declining tendency until the end of 2002, when the amount of TV evening news stories that mentioned Russia was as low as never before in the history of the Vanderbilt News Archive (which has recorded network television news since 1968). The second lowest number of news items dealing with the USSR had been reached in 1973 (277), when still almost twice as much news as in 2003 had been broadcast. An American who watched all the evening news on ABC in 1980 saw 425 USSR-related stories throughout the year, amounting to an average of at least one news report on Russia per day. On the other hand, an American who watched all the evening news on ABC in 2003. saw about 40 news reports mentioning Russia throughout the whole year, which is an average of only three reports per month.

Moreover, the scant amount of attention Russia received throughout the late 1990s in general weighs even less when one subtracts the number of news items that dealt with the Chechen conflict. In 1995, 1996, 1999, 2000, and 2002 about 30 percent of all Russia-related news reported on Russia's war in Chechnya. The two upward drifts in Russia coverage, one throughout 1996 and one throughout 1999 and 2000, are directly linked with an increased number of Chechnya-related news stories, as the red curve clearly shows. In 2002, however, the amount of Chechnya-related news coverage increased whereas the amount of all Russia-related news decreased. Throughout 2003, the Chechen conflict was mentioned rarely, and was replaced by a disproportionate mentioning of Russia's role in the Iraq issue, accounting for a share of about 50 percent of all Russia-related news.

The results of the search for articles in the *New York Times* show similar developments with regard to the quantitative coverage of the Soviet Union/Russia as do the results of the search for evening news on TV.[159] The *New York Times*, as the curve in Fig. 4 shows, published a high number of articles on all kinds of topics with regard to the Soviet Union and the Russians throughout the 1980s. Here, unlike the evening news on TV, the highest number of Russia-related articles was reached with 1400 articles published throughout 1991. Nonetheless, the same phenomenon of extreme decrease in Russia coverage as on TV occurred after the Soviet Union's dissolution. However, the lowest point in Russia coverage in the *New York Times* was reached in 1997 (compared to the TV evening news in 2003). Since then, the number of Russia-related articles increased, but only slightly and in a rather volatile manner. Throughout most of the years since 1995, the Chechen conflict, in the same way as in the evening news on TV, occupied a disproportionately large part of the whole Russia coverage in the *New York Times* (20-30%; for exact numbers of the Lexis Nexis search see Table 5 in the Appendix).

---

[159] The method I used throughout the search in the Lexis-Nexis database was as follows: I decided to use the term "Russia***" combined (through the "OR" tool) with the term "Soviet*" and included results only from the "Headline" option. This combination guaranteed a search for at least one of the following words in all *New York Times* headlines: *Russia, Russian, Russians, Soviets,* and *Soviet* (automatically included a search for the words Soviet Union and USSR). To filter all articles that mentioned the issue of Chechnya, I used the term "chech***" as an additional option combined with the "AND" tool, which guaranteed the search for the words *chechen* and *Chechnya.* To find out in what part of the New York Times the articles were printed, I used the "AND" tool together with one of the following terms "foreign desk", "national desk," "business desk," "cultural desk." To examine how often the terms "crime" and "corruption" occurred in the articles, I used the same method as with the term "chech***."

Fig. 4

Coverage of USSR/Russia-related topics in the *New York Times*

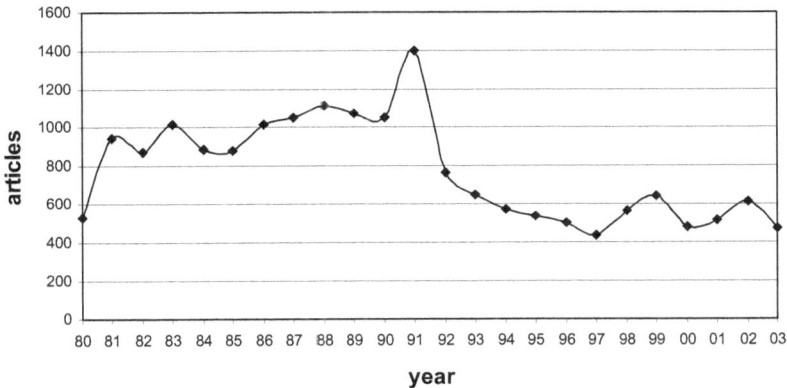

Source: Lexis-Nexis Database

Most of the USSR/Russia-related articles throughout the last two decades had been published within the foreign desk of the *New York Times*. More interesting are the figures regarding the other parts of the newspaper. The percentage of USSR-related articles that Americans could read within the national desk had always been relatively high throughout the early 1980s (well above 5%). A major reason for this, certainly, was the renewed Cold War tension, which was given much attention, because it was of national interest to the United States and hence of major interest to Americans. The highest percentage ever (about 11%) of Soviet Union coverage within the national desk of the *New York Times* was reached in 1985, when Gorbachev appeared and made his first steps of rapprochement. While this percentage declined throughout the second half of the 1980s to about 3 percent in 1990, the percentage of articles that were published in the business desk rose steadily within the same period of time from about 4 percent in 1986 to 16 percent in 1990.

The attention with regard to the Soviet Union, it appears, had shifted considerably to the economic situation there. The percentage of economy-related articles about Russia remained very high throughout the early 1990s when the economic transition in Russia was portrayed in a rosy, but unrealistic fashion by the Clinton administration and most of the American mass media. Though economy-related coverage of Russia reached a low point in the mid-nineties, it has increased again since 1998. In 2003, approximately 18 percent of all Russia-related articles were published in the business desk. This number is out of proportion with the mere four Russia-related articles published in the same year within the national desk.

Russian culture in the early 1980s had been of little interest to the *New York Times*. Throughout the second half of the 1980s, however, the percentage of those Soviet Union-related articles published in the cultural desk rose to an astonishing 8 percent in 1988. Gorbachev's attractiveness and the spirit of "openness" he initiated, one might conclude, have had an effect on the increased interest in Russian culture. This short-lived interest soon started to decrease again, and at the beginning of the 21st century the percentage of articles about Russia in the cultural desk hardly exceeded 3 percent of all Russia-related articles. Whereas in 1988 Americans had the possibility to read 91 articles on Russian culture in the *New York Times*, this number decreased to a mere 20 articles throughout 2003.

There is another interesting tendency in the content of Russia coverage in the *New York Times* throughout the last two decades. Whereas in 1980 only 4.2 percent of all USSR-related articles contained at least one of the words "crime" or "criminal," this percentage had climbed up to 17 percent in 1995 and reached 23.2 percent in 2003. There is a similar tendency in the frequency of the words "corrupt" or "corruption." Whereas the percentage of USSR-related articles containing at least one of the two words rarely exceeded 2 percent throughout the 1980s, the issue was mentioned more and more often throughout the 1990s. The fastest increase in the percentage of articles mentioning corruption occurred from 1998 to 1999. Whereas the issue in 1998 was mentioned in just 7.7 percent of all Russia-related articles, this percentage would almost double just one year later (13.4%). In recent years, however, the use of the words "corrupt" or "corruption" has decreased again by more than half.

Except for the overly optimistic coverage of Russia's economic transformation throughout the early 1990s, the American media leaned toward negative coverage of Russia in the sense that the more negative the news was, the more attention it was given. Yuri Sigov, in 2001, complained about this phenomenon. In *The Russian Journal*, he wrote,

> It's no secret that Russia's image in the United States is still predominantly negative. The U.S. media persistently portrays Russia as a land of crime, general lawlessness, massive human rights violations (especially Chechnya) and persecution of free press. Coupled with its portrayal as an unreliable player on the

world stage, even well-disposed Americans look on Russia with a degree of suspicion and concern.[150]

To sum up, the American media not only during the Cold War but also thereafter produced a distorted image of Russia. This one-sided way of reporting might be a nuisance, but it actually is how most of western journalism functions. More troubling is the fact that Russia moved to the periphery of American public attention. The declining geopolitical importance throughout the early 1990s, the political and societal stagnation and the simultaneous economic recovery under Putin seemed to have produced fewer incentives for the media to mention Russia. Today, Americans hardly see or read anything about their - once daily mentioned - former adversary in the media. This implies that the average American reader or TV viewer is extremely ignorant about Russia and almost completely unaware of current events there. The amount of Russia coverage in the American media today is not enough to change the old stereotyped views of most of the American public and, even worse, might well produce new ones. We can ascertain that because of one-sided and increasingly inadequate Russia coverage in the mass media, the average American could hardly develop the ability to perceive the signals of the cultural code of the Russians, to understand their psychological identity.

Soviet- and Post-Soviet Studies in the United States

Although the first Russian institutes in the U.S. were established in the 1940s at Columbia University (1946), Harvard University (1948), and the University of California Berkeley (1948), when Russia still was an ally, it is no doubt that the Cold War provided enormous stimulus for the expansion of American sovietology. In the 1940s and 1950s, the U.S. government was a driving force in developing Soviet area studies. With the onset of the Cold War, the catalyst for these kinds of efforts was the firm conviction that to "know the enemy" was imperative for U.S. national security. It was against this background that the US Air Force and Harvard's Russian Research Center collaborated to carry out an extensive Interview Project with Soviet refugees to construct a "working model" of Soviet society and delineate a social-psychological profile of its citizens in the event of atom bomb operations against the USSR.[161] A 1991 Social Science Research Council (SSRC) report described the situation:

---

[160] Yuri Sigov, Putin faces odd struggle with U.S. media – Decades of negative mutual news coverage won't change overnight, in: *The Russia Journal*, November 16-22, 2001; Internet Site: <http://www.cdi.org/russia/johnson/5552-4.cfm> (accessed 20 November 2003).
[161] Charles Thomas O'Connell, Social Structure and Sciences: Soviet Studies at Harvard, UCLA Doctoral Dissertation (Department of Sociology), 1990, pp. 332, 353, 385, 429, 430.

The ideological conflicts of the Cold War became an important motive force driving American Soviet studies. Government agencies became an important employer for Soviet studies specialists. ... Because on-the-ground access was limited, close links developed between many American scholars of the region and the American intelligence agencies that were in a position to generate useful information on the Soviet Union.[162]

This kind of collaboration had a negative effect: The government officials' suspicion of everything connected to the Soviet Union that followed from the need to "know the enemy," sometimes extended to individuals and institutions devoted to research on the country. However, the centers would not have flourished as they did without the support of university administrations, the U.S. government and philanthropic foundations (especially the Rockefeller Foundation, the Carnegie Corporation and the Ford Foundation). After the launching of the first Sputnik in October 1957, the Eisenhower Administration persuaded Congress to pass the National Defense Education Act (NDEA) in 1958. It was the basis for substantial support to area studies centers and individuals willing to study languages and areas considered critical to national security. With regard to Soviet area studies, the scope and impact of this funding was considerable.[163] By the end of the 1950s, thirteen major American universities operated institutes, centers, committees, or programs with a focus primarily on Russia. At that time, Columbia's Russian Institute already educated about 200 graduate students and about 100 studied at Harvard's Russian Research Center.[164]

The 1960s and 1970s marked a transitional phase for Soviet area studies. Due to turbulent domestic events, like the Vietnam War, the major foundations shifted their focus from international and foreign area studies to domestic problems. Fortunately, in the 1970s the government created new funding agencies, which guaranteed the survival of the existing centers. The collapse of détente in the late 1970s and the renewed militancy in U.S.-Soviet relations during the first Reagan years had spurred large foundations to turn their attention once again to Soviet area studies. However, by the early 1990s, when Russia had fully opened itself to the West, the major foundations began to redirect a significant proportion of funds previously allocated to U.S. institutions of higher education into the regions themselves, supporting scholars and institutions in the former Soviet Union.

---

[162] Susan Solomon (ed.), *Beyond Sovietology: Essays in Politics and History*, New York, Armonk, 1993, p. 7.
[163] Victoria Bonnell, George Breslauer, Soviet and Post-Soviet Area Studies, Berkley Program in Soviet and Post-Soviet Studies Working Paper Series, Berkley, University of California, 1998, pp. 5-6, 8.
[164] Cyril E. Black, John M. Thomson (eds.), *American Teaching About Russia,* Bloomington, 1959, pp. 53, 56.

In addition, the disappearance of the "enemy" that needs to be "known" and the fiscal crisis that the U.S. government inherited from the Reagan years caused the federal government to reexamine the affordability of continuing contributions to Soviet/Post-Soviet studies, leading to a decline in funding. However, a new source of government funding was made available through the National Security Education Act, which to some extent counterbalanced the threat to the fiscal solvency of post-Soviet studies.[165] The National Security Education Program (NSEP) was designed in 1991 to address the need to increase the ability of Americans to communicate and compete globally by knowing the languages and cultures of world regions that are less-frequently studied.[166] The general financial stringency was compounded by the fiscal crisis experienced by U.S. universities throughout the 1990s, which led to faculty reduction in post-Soviet area studies. The leading centers of research have turned to private-sector fundraising to be more independent of their uncertain base funding.[167]

So far, formal organization of post-Soviet studies in the United States has not changed dramatically since the end of the Cold War. About fifteen major centers in leading universities are funded by the Department of Education. The bulk of published area research continues to be written by scholars associated to the most prominent centers, such as Berkley, Columbia, Harvard, Illinois, Indiana, Michigan, Stanford, UCLA, and the University of Washington. Post-Soviet studies in the United States, however, witnessed a downward trend in student enrollments. During the 1990s, a decline in undergraduate student enrollments in courses on Russian language, history, literature, and politics has taken place on many campuses. Bonnell and Breslauer, in 1996, emphasized that reasons for this trend "are mysterious," but they speculated:

> Historically, enrollments have surged during crucial turning points: at the height of the Cold War in the late 1950s and early 1960s; after the invasion of Afghanistan and the collapse of the limited détente of the 1970s; and during the excitement of the Gorbachev era. But since then, Russia's loss of status as the 'other superpower', and her lack of luster as a place in which to invest one's scholarly dreams and personal fortunes, have led student interests to drift more toward enrollment in courses on other areas, such as East Asia.[168]

At the graduate level, Bonnell and Breslauer observed, interest in pursuing PhDs on postcommunist affairs remained as high as before, but the preference of

---

[165] Bonnell, Breslauer, cited above, pp. 9-10.
[166] NSEP; Internet site: <http://nsep.aed.org/aboutnsep.html>. (accessed 12 October 2003).
[167] Bonnell, Breslauer, cited above, p. 11.
[168] Ibid., p. 15.

specialization shifted from the study of the Soviet Union and/or Russia toward the study of Eastern Europe or non-Russian states of the former Soviet Union.[169]

Despite all of these rather negative tendencies, there have been positive intellectual trends within the field of Soviet/post-Soviet area studies since the late 1980s. Gorbachev's *glasnost'* increasingly diminished the level of data poverty, one of the major difficulties the field had to contend with since its inception. Donald J. Raleigh, in retrospect, called this development "archival revolution."[170] It gave American scholars not only the possibility to find answers with regard to the formerly hidden political sphere, but also to discover new, hitherto neglected cultural dimensions of the Soviet era; including the study of traditions and identities, or themes such as space, time, trust, folklore, collectivism, etc. Students of Russian and Soviet history, like students of Soviet literature, enjoyed the new flows of information from previously closed archives. In area journals, the theoretical repertoire of publications has vastly expanded. Moreover, scholarship in all disciplines of Soviet/post-Soviet area studies increasingly benefited from the new opportunities for collaboration with Soviet and post-Soviet colleagues.[171] Ironically, under improved intellectual conditions the interest in the study of Russia has declined.

Russian Language Study in the United States

> *Language is property, fundamentally belonging to a nation, the most lively expression of its character, the most energetic connection between its people and their culture.*

> -- I. Bluntshli [172]

One of the main cross-cultural communication barriers between Americans and Russians is the language. There is a strong connection and interdependence between the linguistic aspect and the cultural aspect of communication. To understand the meaning of words and expressions in another language that are unique or ambiguous because they stem from a nation's common cultural experience, one has to know this language extraordinarily well. As Barbara Wilson put it, "It's the moment when you stop worrying about grammar and accent, and allow the other language to possess you, to pass through you, to transform you…To speak another language is to lead a parallel life, the better you speak any language, the more fully you live in another culture."[173]

---

[169] Ibid., p. 16.
[170] Donald J. Raleigh, Doing Soviet History: The Impact of the Archival Revolution, in: *Russian Review* 61, 2002, p. 16.
[171] Bonnell, Breslauer, cited above, pp. 20-21, 23.
[172] quoted in: Leontovitsh, cited above, p. 96.
[173] quoted in: Ibid., p. 262.

Nonetheless, the first step toward a better understanding of the people of another culture is to know at least some of their language. Yale Richmond, who was working with Russians for more than twenty-five years observed,

> The Americans most successful in understanding the Russians … are those who speak some Russian. Russian speakers, be they businesspeople, journalists, scholars and scientists, professional or citizen diplomats, all have a significant advantage. Communication may be possible through smiles, hand signals, body language, and interpreters, but the ability to carry on a conversation in Russian raises the relationship to a more meaningful level.[174]

The Modern Language Association (MLA) since 1958 conducted surveys on foreign language enrollments in United States institutions of higher education.[175] According to the MLA data (see Fig. 5),[176] there were two booms in the history of the college-level study of Russian in the U.S.[177] Until the late 1960s, enrollments in Russian language courses were souring. Paul E. Richardson referred to this trend as the "post-Sputnik" boom, after the government on the basis of the NDEA had introduced the National Defense Language Program, which enormously increased the funding for Russian studies.[178] After registrations had dropped throughout the early 1980s, the second boom in Russian language study arrived between the late 1980s and the early 1990s. It was the time when the Soviet Union was in the headlines daily. Nationwide, according to the MLA, there were about 44,600 college-level students of Russian in 1990.

The boom was short-lived By the mid 1990s, as the MLA data show, the number of students of Russian had dropped to less than 25,000. With regard to the reasons for this trend, Richardson in 2001 wrote, "Many reasons have been cited for the 1990s decline: funding changes, lack of job opportunities, fear and loathing of Russia by the US media establishment, etc. But the bottom line is that Russia had lost its 'sex appeal'."[179] He then quoted Jerzy Kolodziej, director of Indiana University's Summer Workshop in Slavic and East European Languages, who said, "The mystery was gone … People get very serious about the unknown, especially if it is powerful and can hurt you." However, according

---

[174] Richmond, cited above, p. 131.
[175] The last survey was carried out in 2002. However, these figures are not yet fully compiled. That is why Fig. 5 only shows the development until 1998, when the last survey before the one in 2002 was conducted.
[176] All MLA data in the text I found in: Richard Brod, Elizabeth B. Welles, Foreign Language Enrollments in United States Institutions of Higher Education, Fall 1998, in: *ADFL Bulletin* 31/2, 2000, pp. 22-29.
[177] Figures of "college-level" study of Russian include undergraduate registrations in 4-year institutions, graduate registrations and two-year college registrations.
[178] Paul E. Richardson, The Decline of Russian, in: *Russian Life*, Jan/Feb 2001, p. 43.
[179] Richardson, cited above, p. 43.

to Benjamin Rifkin, director of University of Madison's Russian program, the 1990s decline has to be understood in a larger perspective. The era of the late 1980s, he said, "was a blip, an unusual one ... In the history of Russian language study, that was an anomaly." Enrollments, he emphasized in 2001, were "very parallel to ... the late 1970s and early 1980s and through much of the rest of the century since WWII."[180]

This observation might be correct if one looks at the pure figures regarding the enrollments in Russian language courses on the college-level over the years. It should not be overlooked, however, that the share of Russian language registrations in total registrations of the fourteen most commonly taught languages in the U.S. was much lower in 1998 (2.0%), than in 1980 (3.8%), (see Table 6 in the Appendix). Whereas the Russian language in 1968 took the fourth place within the most commonly taught languages (behind Spanish, French, and German), it fell to sixth place until 1980 and to eighth place until 1998. Notably, study of Italian, Japanese and Chinese surged as Russian went on the decline. Russian language registrations from 1960 to 1995 followed over-exaggerated upward and downward trends experienced by overall language registrations in general (see Fig. 5 and Fig. 6). Troubling, however, is the fact that the number of students studying Russian declined from 1995 to 1998, while the aggregate number of all foreign language registrations increased. According to the MFL data, U.S. institutions of higher education in 1998 witnessed the highest number of overall foreign language enrollments, but the lowest number in Russian language enrollments ever.

---

[180] Richardson, cited above, p. 44.

Fig. 5

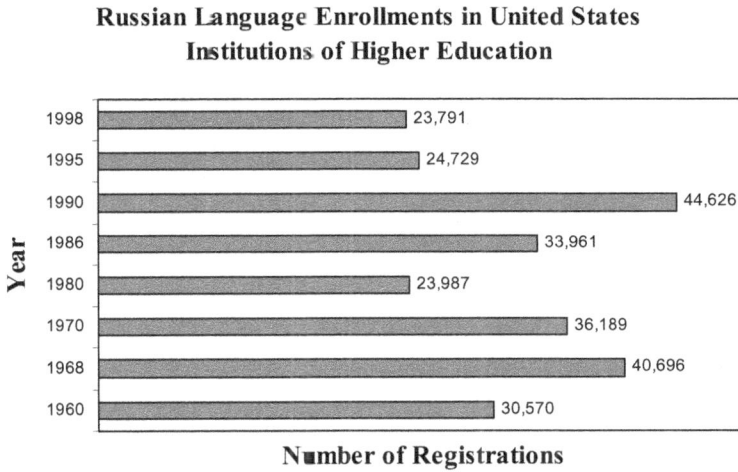

Russian Language Enrollments in United States Institutions of Higher Education

Year	Number of Registrations
1998	23,791
1995	24,729
1990	44,626
1986	33,961
1980	23,987
1970	36,189
1968	40,696
1960	30,570

Fig. 6

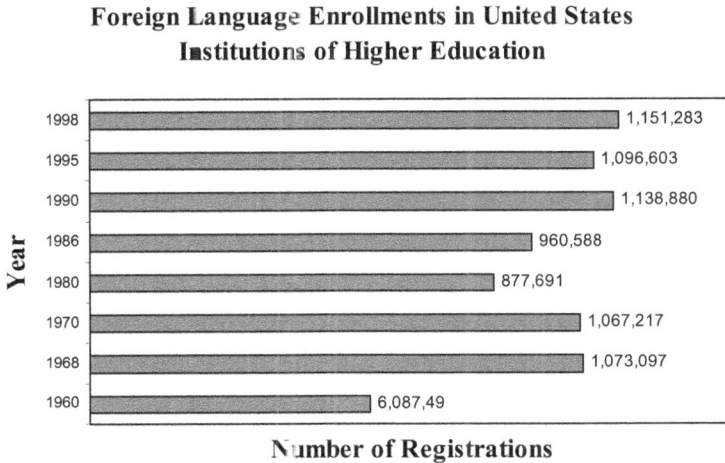

Foreign Language Enrollments in United States Institutions of Higher Education

Year	Number of Registrations
1998	1,151,283
1995	1,096,603
1990	1,138,880
1986	960,588
1980	877,691
1970	1,067,217
1968	1,073,097
1960	6,087,49

It is important to note, that the decline did not come to a halt, although the federal government under the NSEP act of 1991 was funding the study of less commonly taught languages, from areas of the world where the U.S. has particular national security interests, including Russia. Students of Russian, interestingly, have benefited quite disproportionately from this program because Americans with Russian language experience were increasingly needed for empty positions not only in the private sector or the nonprofit sector, but in the government sector as well.[181] Russian remains one of the languages on the list of NSEP's critical languages that enjoy special emphasis in funding.[182]

The 1990s have witnessed a parallel downturn in high school and middle school Russian language study enrollments. Since 1984, the Committee on College and Pre-College Russian (CCPCR) has periodically polled pre-college Russian language study programs throughout the United States. The CCPCR was created as the result of the 1983 Report of the National Committee for Russian Language Study[183], which noted that "enrollments in the Russian language have dropped more precipitously than those in any other major modern language."[184] The CCPCR data, according to John Schillinger, who organizes the annual surveys, lack accuracy because some of the schools with Russian language programs did not respond regularly to the census. However, the collected figures show general trends regarding the interest in Russian language study on the pre-college level. Whereas in the mid 1980s, the number of schools never exceeded 200 and the number of students of Russian remained under 8,000, these figures had doubled by 1989 when the census witnessed a unique peak, listing more than 400 schools and almost 18,000 students nationwide. Since then, the interest has steadily decreased until 1999, when less than 100 schools with less than 5,000 students responded to the census.[185]

According to the CCPCR data, the downward trend seemed to have reversed, with more and more schools responding since 2000. Schillinger, however, points out that these figures are not reliable and that what one can truly rely on is the list of actual schools whose Russian language programs have been terminated.[186] These data show that from 1998 to 2003, 144 pre-college

---

[181] Richardson, cited above, p. 44.

[182] NSEP; Internet site: <http://nsep.aed.org/aboutnsep.html> (accessed 12 October 2003).

[183] The Committee of Russian Language Study is composed of representatives of the American Association for the Advancement of Slavic Studies (AAASS), the American Association of Teachers of Slavic and East European Languages (ATSEEL), and the American Council of Teachers of Russian (ACTR).

[184] CCPCR; Internet site: <http://www.american.edu/research/CCPCR/infoorg.htm> (accessed 20 October 2003).

[185] All available CCPCR pre-college level data from 1984 to 2001 I received from John Schillinger via e-mail in November, 2003. Only the data from 1996 to 2001 are listed on the CCPCR website: <http://www.american.edu/research/CCPCR/stats.htm.> (accessed 20 October 2003).

[186] I received this information from John Schillinger in November, 2003.

programs have been terminated[187]. Specifically, from 1998 – 2000, 127 programs were lost. While the pace of termination has decreased considerably thereafter, Schillinger in 2002 stressed that "the impact of such significant overall losses on a national scale since 1998 is overwhelming." He went on, complaining, "On a state-by-state basis, the picture is grim. In eleven states ... only one pre-college Russian program has been reported to date (less than half of these states have previously reported more than one school ...). Fifteen states ... to the best of our knowledge now have no Russian programs at the pre-college level."[188]

If one adds the data from the most current surveys on Russian language study (the MLA data for the college level/the CCPCR data for the pre-college level) it appears that as a critical foreign language for U.S. security interests, Russian is itself in critical condition. The decline in Russian language study throughout the 1990s has led to the shutdown of several Russian language study programs and the sharp curtailment of others. The "crisis" of the 1990s led many programs to think about how to make themselves more attractive. As Richardson observed, "...it is a generally shared conclusion that the most important thing that educators and others can do to foster more Russian language study is to create greater awareness of Russian culture, history, literature and the arts. It is an interest in these subjects that will spur students to the hard work of learning Russian." Moreover, he found that "study abroad programs are also taking on new dimensions" since "the collapse of the USSR has spawned many new opportunities for study of Russian culture and language *within* Russia."[189]

---

[187] All 144 pre-college Russian programs that have been terminated from 1998-2003 (last updated on September 23, 2003) are listed on the CCPCR website: <http://www.american.edu/research/CCPCR/Terminated%20programs01.htm.> (accessed 20 November 2003).

[188] John Schillinger: "Results and Implications of the Fall 2001 CCPCR Census of Pre-College Russian Programs: The Decline Slows, But Now Is the Time for LOCAL Action", article published on the CCPCR website: <http://www.american.edu/research/CCPCR/articlefall2001.htm> (accessed 20 October 2003).

[189] Richardson, cited above, p. 46.

13. American-Russian Encounters

In the long run we will only have a good relationship
with the Russian Government when we have
a good relationship with the Russian people.

-- Warren Christopher (1995)[190]

The historian J.D. Parks, for the period from 1917 to the 1970s, divided the cultural relationship between the two nations into four periods: First, there was the pre-Stalinist period of the twenties and early thirties, when cultural contacts "were surprisingly full and free." Although ordinary Soviet citizens were rarely permitted to travel abroad, "Soviet cultural representatives, technical delegations and artistic exhibits visited American cities ..., and American tourists, technicians, businessmen and cultural figures reciprocated the visits in large numbers." The second period was marked by Stalin's dictatorship. In the course of his antiforeign campaign during the late thirties, "the free and easy contacts began to diminish." Stalin after the Second World War "increasingly isolated the Soviet people from outside contacts," and Washington in the face of Cold War tensions "responded by erecting its own barriers to contacts with communists." By the early 1950s, the cultural relationship had reached an impasse. The post-Stalinist fifties constitute the third period, when the new Soviet rulers broadened Soviet contacts with Europe and Asia, but "a reluctant and suspicious Washington provided little encouragement or support for similar contacts with the United States." As the cultural climate slowly thawed, both sides signed an official exchange pact in 1958, which marked the beginning of the fourth period with numerous organized exchanges under official auspices.[191]

After the failure of détente in the late seventies, however, cultural relations had reached another impasse, when the cultural agreement negotiated biannually since 1958 was not renewed in 1980, and not renegotiated until 1984. The Reagan administration had little interest in developing non-political contacts. It was a time when there was almost no cultural contact between Americans and Russians.[192] Throughout most of the Cold War years both Moscow and Washington used cultural relations as a means to an end. A major objective was to infuse "ideas and information" into the society of the adversary. The fact that cultural relations represented a means, not an end, necessarily limited the extent to which the two nations could enter into an unfettered

---

[190] former Secretary of State Warren Christopher; *New York Times*, 7 May 1995.
[191] J.D. Parks, *Culture, Conflict and Coexistence – American-Soviet Cultural Relations, 1917-1958*, Jefferson (U.S.), London (U.K.), McFarland, 1983, pp. 2-3.
[192] Boyle, cited above, p. 211.

relationship that characterized the interaction between American citizens and those of Western nations.

Gorbachev's overtures in the mid-1980s paved the way for an unprecedented scope of cultural exchanges between the two nations. Cultural relations in Washington's and Moscow's eyes soon stopped to be a mere means to an end, and started to serve a noble purpose, namely, to exchange information and experiences and to achieve real mutual understanding between the people on both sides. A decade later, these cultural contacts have reached such a level that Yale Richmond thought the time was ripe for a book specifically intended for Americans who anticipate interaction with Russians in an exchange, social, or professional setting. He wrote his book *From Nyet to Da – Understanding the Russians* (1996) to support Americans in their efforts to communicate with Russians by helping them to understand the culture of their former adversaries.

Leontovitsh recognized several spheres of cross-cultural contact; including diplomatic activities, professional contacts, trade and business, international exchanges and study or travel abroad.[193] The last two decades experienced an astonishing amount of people-to-people contacts. Due to this fact, and also because many of these contacts are organized on an informal level (which makes it difficult to find sufficient information), it is impossible to give a complete overview of American-Russian encounters. This study rather concentrates on major initiatives or projects and gives only examples for the developments in U.S.-Russian relations on a people-to-people level.

Diplomatic Activities

On the highest level of diplomacy, the tensions throughout the Cold War kept direct contacts between American and Soviet political leaders extremely low. From 1943 to 1984, there were only nineteen U.S.-Soviet leadership meetings. On the contrary, throughout the mere eighteen years from 1985 to 2003, the presidents of the Soviet Union/Russia and the United States met about forty times. The nineties have witnessed the establishment of many active government-to-government working groups on technology, energy, health, fisheries, the environment, etc., which are still active today. One of the largest, most influential and famous joint working groups during the Clinton Administration was the Gore-Chernomyrdin Commission, in which high-ranking American and Russian diplomats discussed cooperation in such fields as economy, science (especially joint space exploration), and engineering. The most important joint diplomatic endeavor today is the U.S.-Russian Counter-Terrorism Working Group. Moreover, since 2001, the Nixon Center has regularly invited prominent American and Russian groups of influential

---

[193] Leontovitsh, cited above, p. 51.

decisionmakers and intellectuals to hold the U.S.-Russian Dialogue, where both sides discuss the history and the current state of the U.S.-Russian relationship.[194]

An example of outstanding "citizen diplomacy" was set by the Center for Citizen Initiatives (CCI)[195] in 1983, when the organization's president Sharon Tennison led a handful of ordinary American citizens on a mission to challenge the barriers of fear and mistrust between the two Superpowers. The "Citizen Diplomats," as they called themselves, wanted to create an alternative to the arms race and open communications between the U.S. and the USSR. During the following years, the CCI organized travel to the USSR for thousands of Americans with the intention to build human connections with counterpart Soviet citizens. For about three weeks each of these American travelers took to the Soviet streets in search of citizens willing to communicate with them and, according to the CCI, were invited by Soviet citizens into their schools, hospitals and apartments despite surveillance and decades of repression. During the politically tense seven-year period prior to the implosion of the Soviet Union in 1991, CCI facilitated tens of thousands of face-to-face interactions between Soviet and American citizens. As the CCI emphasizes, "American travelers were forever changed as a result of going to the enemy country and finding no enemy at home."

After they returned from their trips, the "Citizen Diplomats," as they had previously pledged, performed six months of public education in the United States. Hundreds of thousands of Americans learned about citizens of the USSR through the U.S. travelers' presentations in schools, universities, Rotary Clubs, city hall meetings, churches, or professional associations, but also through newspaper articles, television and radio interviews. In the meantime, the Soviets Meet Middle America (SMMA) program was launched to bring American and Soviet citizens together "around the kitchen table" in American homes. They stayed in over 800 American homes, visited more than 260 American cities and towns, numerous American institutions, and were covered in over 1,000 newspapers and interviewed on television and radio in every city they visited.

Numerous travel and exchange programs, environmental initiatives, agricultural projects, sister city relationships and personal friendships were born as a result of both projects. While SMMA was meant for just two years, the Citizen Diplomacy Travel Program completed its mission and closed in 1991. CCI, thereafter, shifted its attention to economic development in Russia.

---

[194] The Nixon Center is a non-partisan public policy institution established by former President Richard Nixon shortly before his death in 1994. Major programs of The Nixon Center include the Chinese Studies Program, National Security Program, Regional Strategic Program, and U.S.-Russian Relations Program. All information on programs, events and activities of the Nixon Center are available on Internet Site: <http://www. nixoncenter.org>.
[195] CCI is a non-profit organization, which has been established in 1983 and in the first two years was self-funded by the handful of volunteers who created the organization.

Interestingly, in 1983, according to CCI, "members of U.S. government agency visited CCI leaders requesting them to disband and remove themselves from international activity, so as not to get in the way of real diplomatic efforts with the USSR." However, since the early nineties, the organization has been courted by the U.S. government exactly because of the knowledge and contacts it had established throughout the years. When the United States began funding technical assistance for Russia in 1993, USAID asked CCI to assist in the development of small business in Russia and immediately started to fund the organization's programs.[196]

In 1999, the Open World Program, also called Russian Leadership Program (RLP), was launched on the initiative of James Billington, renowned as a prominent Russia scholar as well as heading the Library of Congress. It was the result of discussions between Billington and members of Congress led by Senator Ted Stevens (AK) on ways to increase mutual understanding between Russia and the United States and to support Russia's efforts to strengthen its democratic reforms.[197] The program holds the distinction of being the first-ever grant-making program and the only exchange program established within the legislative branch. Since its creation, the Open World Program has received grants totaling $51 million from the U.S. Congress. Under the auspices of the Center for Russian Leadership Development at the Library of Congress almost 7,000 Russian participants from all levels of government and from across the political spectrum have been hosted in the United States.[198] From the very beginning, the Open World Program has aimed to create ties and foster better understanding between Russia and the United States by inviting young prominent Russian politicians and other federal, regional and local officials. The program offers them insight into the American political and economic systems and educates them about the complexities of American democracy. It focuses its work on eight areas: the rule of law, economic development, women as leaders, health, education reforms, the environment, federalism and youth issues.[199]

A central element of the Open World experience is the homestay. Participants for some or most of their local visit are placed in private homes and are often paired off with hosts that had similar occupations. This, according to RLP's 2000 Annual Report, "enabled them to observe firsthand American-style

---

[196] All citations and information on CCI's history and programs were taken from the CCI website: <http://www.ccisf.org> (accessed 10 December 2003).
[197] Center for Russian Leadership Development – Annual Report 2002, p. 1; Internet Site: <http://www.rlp.gov/docs/report02.pdf.> (accessed 17 December 2003).
[198] Open World Leadership Center, Fact Sheet 2003; Internet Site: <http://www.rlp.gov /docs/fact_sheet _en_071103.pdf> (accessed 17 December 2003).
[199] Claire Bigg, "U.S.-Russia Program Aims to Open World", article reprinted with the permission by *The St.Petersburg Times*, Center for Russian Leadership Development at the Library of Congress, posted on April 15, 2003; Internet Site: <http://www.openworld.gov/index-e.htm> (accessed 8 October 2003).

family dynamics and household management, participate in typically American social, community, religious, and recreational events, and develop personal and professional ties with their hosts." The report further reads, "Host families benefited in turn from the opportunity to learn about Russian geography, history, culture, and politics from some of the country's most promising future leaders. In 2000, a total of 547 host families in 46 states welcomed RLP participants into their homes."[200] Almost 60 percent of the Open World delegates are federal, regional or local government officials. In addition, over 500 Russian judges and legal professionals have been hosted in U.S. courts and communities as part of Open World visits focused on the rule of law. The Russian delegates come from all of the Russian Federation's 89 regions and represent 55 ethnic groups. On the other side, over 900 American communities in all 50 states and the District of Columbia have hosted them.[201]

Due to the Open World initiative, ties between the members of Congress and Russian parliament are enhancing. In 2000, for example, the RLP placed special emphasis on inviting members of the Federation Council and the State Duma – the upper and the lower houses, respectively, of Russia's Federal Assembly. Under the parliamentary program a total of 14 Federal Council members, 92 State Duma deputies, 39 parliamentary aids, and 4 ministry-level officials traveled to the United States. Nearly all the parliamentary groups were hosted by a member of Congress or a governor. A total of 21 congressmen, 4 senators, and 5 governors hosted delegations in their constituencies. The Russian politicians campaigned door-to-door with political candidates, visited police stations, firehouses, and hospitals, toured businesses, farms, soup kitchens, and medical clinics, or interacted with students at all educational levels. They had working meetings and round tables with mayors, state agency officials, newspaper editors, businesspeople, civic leaders, and nonprofit heads.[202] From the beginning of 2001, over thirty delegations from Russia's Federal Assembly visited the United States. Interparliamentary "Duma-Congress" and "Senate-Council of the Federation" groups have been created, and demonstrate the program's success in building parliamentary ties. In 2001, Speaker of the House, D. Hastert, and Democratic Leader R. Gephardt visited Russia. In 2002, Speaker of the Duma, G. Seleznev, visited the U.S. and signed a memorandum on cooperation between the State Duma and the House of Representatives. Other prominent U.S. Congressmen have visited Russia since then.[203]

---

[200] Russian Leadership Program – FY 2000 Report to the U.S. Congress, Internet Site: <www.rlp.gov/ docs/report00.pdf> (accessed 17 December 2003).

[201] Open World Leadership Center, Fact Sheet 2003; Internet Site: <http://www.rlp.gov /docs/fact_sheet _en_071103.pdf> (accessed 17 December 2003).

[202] Russian Leadership Program – FY 2000 Report to the U.S. Congress, pp. 10-12; Internet Site: <www.rlp.gov/docs/report00.pdf> (accessed December 2003).

[203] See the website of the Russian Embassy to the United States, Internet Site: <http://www. russianembassy.org/embassy/rus-usa.htm> (accessed 17 December 2003).

There is no doubt that Open World is an example of promoting greater understanding between Russians and Americans. A key premise of the program, according to RPL's 2000 Annual Report, is that "emphasizing face-to-face encounters will help dispel the negative, Cold War-era stereotypes that many Russians and Americans hold." Data from a survey of RLP 2000 participants indicate that 82 percent are more ready to cooperate with American leaders as a result of the exchange.[204] Although the program is intended for Russians to learn from their American counterpart, its emphasis on small-group programming, home hosting, and informal program formats gives their participating American members unmatched opportunities to develop personal and professional ties with their Russian guests and to learn about their homeland as well. The contacts established in the United States have led to some reciprocal visits of Americans to Russia and will lead to more in the future. Moreover, the initiative received considerable media coverage in the U.S. and Russia. For example, the total of newspaper articles published in both countries throughout 1999 numbered over 500. CNN, in that year presented a television special on the program.[205] Soon after Billington and Stevenson had visited St.Petersburg during the 300th anniversary celebrations in early 2003, they announced the expansion of the Open World Program to the cultural sphere, starting with visits of prominent Russian artists to leading American cultural institutions.[206]

Professional Contacts

The most well-known joint professional endeavors undertaken by Americans and Russians in the last twenty years, probably, are the human spaceflight cooperative activities involving the Space Shuttle-Space Station Mir dockings and the International Space Station (ISS). Although the United States and the Soviet Union had started to cooperate on the exploration of outer space already at the beginning of the 1960s, intense political and military competition between the two countries severely limited the duration and scope of such activities. After all, during the Cold War both sides competed against each other as archrivals in the "space race." Due to the improved relationship during the last few years of the Cold War period, new opportunities and new incentives occurred for the United States and other countries to cooperate with the Soviet Union in space science, space application, and human space flight.

In 1987, an agreement on joint U.S.-Soviet space exploration was signed, which owed much of its restrictive provisions to the 1970s experience, but

---

[204] Russian Leadership Program – FY 2000 Report to the U.S. Congress, pp. 10-12, 14; Internet Site: <www.rlp.gov/docs/report00.pdf> (accessed 17 December 2003).
[205] The Library of Congress – Open World 1999 Leadership Program Final Report, Internet Site: <http://www.rlp.gov/docs/report99.pdf> (accessed 17 December 2003).
[206] Bigg, cited above.

differed importantly from previous agreements. It included an annex with a list of 16 approved areas of cooperation. The agreement reworked the previously existing Joint Working Group (JWG) structure and authorized the formation of groups in space biology and medicine, astronomy and astrophysics, space physics, solar system exploration, and earth sciences. The JWGs were expected to meet at least annually. The collapse of the USSR put aside all worries of program managers that the political linkage could work to disrupt cooperative undertakings, as events in Afghanistan and Poland had during 1982-1987.

When in 1992 a new civil space agreement was concluded at the first summit between Bush and Yeltsin, for the first time since the joint experiences in the 1970s, the prospect of cooperation in human spaceflight was acknowledged. The agreement foresaw Space Shuttle and Mir Space Station missions involving the participation of U.S. astronauts and Russian cosmonauts and explicitly raised the possibility of working together in the exploration of Mars, a project to be called the Mars '94 mission, which brought together American and Russian experts as key players in the International Mars Exploration Working Group. The 1992 agreement, moreover, sanctioned a very significant increase in activity across the entire range of cooperative space science and applications projects between NASA (National Aeronautics and Space Administration), the Russian Space Agency (RSA), the Russian Academy of Science, and several other Russian agencies. Since 1993, on the diplomatic front, a series of contacts between the two governments, between NASA and RSA, and between the members of the Gore-Chernomyrdin Commission led to a set of agreements regarding Russia's participation in the space station partnership and its role in the development of the International Space Station (ISS). Furthermore, during the 1990s, the JWG structure had been expanded and cooperation between American and Russian members had proceeded relatively smoothly. Both sides agreed on new joint scientific projects, such as the joint study of the Sun and Pluto, called "Fire and Ice."[207]

During the late nineties, Americans and Russians participated in shared space station flights. The first American astronaut to be sent to work on a Mir mission in 1995 was Norman Thagard. It appeared that Russians and Americans had overcome monumental differences and competition, moving into a truly cooperative spirit in the manned space station program. A March 1995 *Space News* article read,

> With a Russian folk song blaring in the background, U.S. astronaut Norman Thagard floated in the Mir space station, March 16, opening a new era of

---

[207] U.S. Congress, Office of Technology Assessment, U.S.-Russian Cooperation in Space, OTA-ISS-618, Washington, DC: U.S. Government Printing Office, April 1995, pp. 47-52; Internet Site: <http://www.wws.princeton.edu/cgi-bin/byteserv.prl/~ota/disk1/1995/9546.PDF> (accessed 18 December 2003).

cooperation between former Cold War rivals to pave the way toward a jointly operated station later this decade. ... He was greeted by a hug and a kiss on the cheek from cosmonaut Helena Kondakova, along with a traditional present of bread and salt.[208]

Despite the unsteady nature of the U.S. and Russian cooperation in space-related enterprises, mainly owing to cultural barriers[209] and the chronic lack of financing on the Russian side, experts from both countries did a large amount of work together in assembling the ISS structure. Since the end of 2000, seven crews have lived on the space station, including 10 Americans and 10 Russians.[210] Behind the scenes, an enormous number of American and Russian diplomats, scientists, technicians, engineers, and other professionals have come together to accomplish common goals. NASA, for example, has a large presence in the Moscow area today, with offices at the U.S. Embassy, the Moscow Mission Control Center, and the Russian Space Agency.[211]

Besides the partnership in the space program, there are numerous other fields where Americans and Russians experience professional contacts. Often, these projects are funded by the U.S. government, but are carried out by NGOs. Many of them experienced a boom in the nineties, after the Freedom Support Act provided for assistance to Russia in its economic and democratic transformation process. Even in the sector of NGO cooperation, professionals on both sides are working together. The Initiative for Social Action and Renewal in Eurasia (ISAR), for example, is a nongovernmental organization, founded in 1983, that operates as an international association of NGOs with members in Moscow, Novosibirsk and Vladivostok. ISAR's mission is to strengthen grassroots organizations in the U.S. and Eurasia, including Russia. In order to achieve this mission, ISAR initiates and supports communication and cooperation among NGOs and receives funds not only from private donors and philanthropic foundations, but also from U.S. government agencies, such as USAID.[212]

The private nonprofit organization CONNECT/US-Russia (formerly CONNECT/US-USSR) was founded in 1984 by two American women from Minneapolis to promote knowledge and understanding between the citizens of

---

[208] Harwood, William; quoted in: Joan M. Abelman, Challenges to U.S.-Russian Cooperation in the Manned Space Program – A Research Report , Air War College Air University, Alabama, April 1996, p. 2.

[209] A thorough discussion on the cultural barriers American and Russian experts were confronted with during their joint efforts in the space station program throughout the 1990s can be found in: Abelman, cited above, pp. 20-28.

[210] Information on the history of ISS crews can be found on the NASA website: <http://spaceflight.nasa.gov/home/index.html> (accessed 18 December 2003).

[211] U.S. Embassy to Moskow; Internet site: <http://www.usembassy. ru/mission/nasa.php> (accessed 15 December 15 2003).

[212] ISAR, Internet Site: <http://www.isar.org> (accessed 14 November 2003).

the United States and the former Soviet Union. Sponsored by the State Department's Bureau of Educational and Cultural Affairs since 1995, CONNECT facilitates homestay-based, three-to-five week practical training opportunities for local government officials, legal professionals, nongovernmental organization leaders and other professionals from Russia and the other NIS countries.[213] Since 1993, the Center for Citizen Initiatives, on a much larger scale, receives USAID grants for its numerous initiatives with regard to Russia. CCI, after completion of its Citizen Diplomacy project has dedicated itself to supporting Russia in its economic transformation. The organization's Productivity Enhancement Program (PEP), a multi-million dollar program funded by the U.S. State Department, is widely regarded as the leading edge program for business training in Russia. Throughout the last ten years, CCI has graduated more than 4,000 Russian entrepreneurs from U.S.-based business management internships. Currently, it manages over 20,000 volunteers, who train these interns across 45 U.S. states. The organization has seven Russian partner offices that oversee the work of over 50 satellite operations in the regions of Russia.[214]

The American Russian Center (ARC) at the University of Alaska in Anchorage is another example of a U.S. government-funded non-profit organization promoting Russia's transition to a free market economy. Focused on the Russian Far East, the ARC trains entrepreneurs, business managers and government leaders from this region. Since it began operations in 1993, the ARC has conducted over 1,200 business courses and seminars. It operates eight business development centers in the Russian Far East region.[215] The Alliance of American and Russian Women (AARW) was founded in 1991 with the specific goal of assisting Russian women to make the transition to a market economy. Since 1993, AARW has trained more than 1,700 women in business skills seminars and women's empowerment seminars in the Russian North-West region. With financial support from government agencies, this NGO organizes exchanges and business partnerships among American and Russian businesswomen.[216]

The American Russian Law Institute (ARLI) is a non-profit legal and public policy research and advisory organization dedicated to promoting legal reform in Russia. Under the leadership of Emnuel E. Zeltser, chairman of ARLI, Russian and American specialists had taken part in major litigations in Russia, the U.S. and other countries throughout the 1990s. These cases generally involved the Russian bank's interaction with the Western financial system and

---

[213] CONNECT; Internet Site: <http://www.connectusrussia.org> (accessed 3 November 2003).
[214] CCI; Internet site: <http://www.ccisf.org> (accessed 10 December 2003).
[215] ARC; Internet site: <http://www.arc.uaa.alaska.edu/index.htm> (accessed 18 December 2003).
[216] AARW; Internet site: <http://www.aarwomen.org/english/welcome.html> (accessed 15 October 2003).

particularly with the Bank of New York. In 1992, at the request of the then Russian Minister of Justice, Zeltser and his American colleagues participated in drafting the new Russian banking legislation. A year later, in conjunction with the Academy of Jurisprudence of the Ministry of Justice of Russia and the Law School of Pittsburg University, they translated and codified the first official English language codification of Russian trade and commercial law.[217]

In 2001, at the initiative of Presidents Bush and Putin, the Russian-American Media Entrepreneurship Dialog (RAMED) was launched as a forum for Russian and American media executives to examine recent developments and current challenges facing the Russian media. Through the Dialogue's mechanisms, leading print and broadcast media professionals from the U.S. and Russia examined issues of business and the legal environment. They sought answers to developing and strengthening a stable, varied and independent media sector in Russia.[218] Four working groups have been formed to address industry constraints and solutions in the areas of industry structure, content, economic base, and technology.[219] RAMED includes an internship program at U.S. stations for Russian regional television and radio broadcasters and high-level roundtables for Russian and U.S. media people, who discuss issues such as legislation and regulation, international co-production and production financing, trends in advertising, and the challenges to broadcasting from new technologies.[220]

Even in such an unnoticed field as forestry, American and Russian professionals are cooperating successfully. The USDA (United States Department of Agriculture) Forest Service has worked with Russian partners since the mid-nineties to promote sustainable forestry practices and address forest health issues. Since Russia has the largest forest resource of any country in the world, these joint efforts have genuine global significance. The focus in Russia is on Central Siberia's and the Russian Far East's extensive forests. Many factors have made this area vulnerable, like forest fires, damaging windstorms and selective logging. Mainly funded by USAID, the USDA Forest Service carries out a series of training workshops, exchanges, and demonstration projects so that both countries have the opportunity to learn from each other. Since the early nineties, the USDA Forest Service and the Russian Aerial Fire Service have participated in a Wildland Firefighter Exchange Program. The

---

[217] ARLI; Internet site: <http://russianlaw.org> (accessed 18 December 2003).

[218] Internews; Internet site: <http://www.internews.ru/internews/ramed/indexe.html> (accessed 23 November 2003).

[219] Whitehouse Office of the Press Secretary, Fact Sheet: Media Entrepreneurship Dialogue, May 24, 2002; Internet Site: < http://www.whitehouse.gov/news/releases/2002/05/20020524-14.html (accessed 19 December 2003).

[220] see article "Russian-American Media Entrepreneurship Dialogue Follow-On," September 12, 2003; Interenet Site: <http://www.internews.org/news/2003/20030912_ru.html> (accessed 19 December 2003).

primary goal is to strengthen both countries' fire programs through the exchange of information and technologies and to instruct the Russian crews in organization, equipment use and safety. For example, after a delegation of U.S. specialists had traveled to Russia in 1999, they recommended the purchase of critical radio equipment. In the following year, a shipment of a large number of the latest two-way radios and associated equipment to their Russian colleagues was completed.[221]

Trade and Business Relations

U.S.-Soviet economic ties were very limited during the Cold War. National security and foreign policy restrictions (including the Jackson Vanik amendment restrictions) functioned as barriers to normal trade relations between the two superpowers. Furthermore, Soviet economic policies of central planning tightly controlled foreign trade and prohibited investment. After the Soviet Union collapsed, the reforms of the successive Russian leaders brought about the liberalization of foreign trade and investment. Despite expanded U.S.-Russian trade relations, the flow of trade and investment between the two nations remains very low.[222] Although U.S. imports have increased appreciably from 1992 to 2002 (thirteen-fold from $0.5 billion to $6.8 billion), it is not even a fourth of what the U.S. imported from Germany in 2002 ($28,8 billion). Throughout the nineties, U.S. exports to Russia had never exceeded $4 billion annually. Compared to the U.S. exports to the relatively small Germany ($21.2 billion), this figure appears quite low. Despite the general increase in trade, Russia still accounts for only 0.5 percent of U.S. imports and 0.4 percent of U.S. exports.[223]

U.S. imports from and exports to Russia embrace only few commodity categories. About 70 percent of what Russia sold to the United States in 2001, were precious stones, inorganic chemicals, mineral fuels, aluminum, iron, steel, and fish. Over 50 percent of U.S. exports to Russia mainly consisted of meat (mostly poultry), machinery (mostly parts for oil and gas production equipment), art and antiques, electrical machinery, and optical equipment. Although U.S. direct investment has increased since the disintegration of the Soviet Union, the levels are far below their expected potential. However, in 2001, the United States was Russia's largest source of foreign direct investments. American investors had concentrated in the transportation, energy, communications and

---

[221] USDA Forest Service; Internet site: <http://www.fs.fed.us/global/globe/europe/russia.htm> (accessed 25 October 2003).
[222] William H. Cooper, Permanent Normal Trade Relations (PNTR) Status for Russia and U.S.-Russian Economic Ties, CRS Report for Congress, Congressional Research Service, The Library of Congress, Order Code RS21123, January 28, 2002, p.3.
[223] Source: U.S. Department of Commerce, International Trade Administration; Internet site: <http://www.ita.doc.gov> (accessed 21 December 2003).

engineering sectors.[224] As unsatisfactory as U.S.-Russian trade relations still might be, there is no doubt that since the end of the Cold War Americans and Russians have forged an unprecedented number of business contacts.

Not long ago, Russian and American business communities established the Russian- American Business Dialogue, a forum where business interests can be raised with the respective governments. It is steered by the U.S.-Russian Business Council (USRBC), the American Chamber of Commerce (Amcham) and the Russian Union of Industrialists and Entrepreneurs. As a business-to-business mechanism, the Dialogue is intended to expand contact between the two private sectors. Shortly after it was launched, Bush and Putin on the Genoa Summit, in 2001, welcomed the initiative.[225] Since then, both governments are supporting the Business Dialogue and within the framework of the Foundation for Cooperation committed themselves "to working with the private sectors of our countries to realize the full potential of our economic interaction."[226]

Another important part of the new structure in economic relations between Russia and the U.S. is the so-called Russian American Pacific Partnership (RAPP).[227] It is a bilateral forum that engages the private sector and government structures to resolve barriers to business and commerce between the U.S. West Coast and the Russian Far East. In 2003, RAPP held its eighth annual meeting. More than 250 public and private sector representatives from both countries met in the Siberian city of Yuzhno-Sakhalinsk to discuss current and future fields of bilateral economic cooperation. While the U.S. West Coast states represent one of the leading economic regions in the world, the Russian Far East is rich in resources and human capital with prospects for tremendous economic growth. RAPP covers numerous fields of cooperation between the two regions, such as forestry, ecology and mining, fisheries, agriculture, transportation, and tourism. It has especially focused on the energy sector. Sakhalin oil and gas projects represent the core of American-Russian business cooperation in the region, including joint ventures.[228] Sakhalin Island has become one of the most important regions in Russia for U.S. commercial activity. Because U.S.

---

[224] Cooper, cited above, pp. 3-4.

[225] White House Office of the Press Secretary, Fact Sheet on the Russian-American Business Dialogue, September 27, 2003; Internet site: <http://usinfo.state.gov>. (accessed 13 October 2003).

[226] The White House Office of Press Secretary, "Joint Declaration on New US-Russia Relationship," PDQ database, Date: 20020524; Internet site: <http://www.whitehouse.gov /news/releases/ 2001/11/20011113-4.html> (November 26, 2003).

[227] RAPP was formerly known as the U.S. West Coast – Russian Far East Ad-Hoc Working Group.

[228] Joint Report of the Eighth Annual Meeting of the Russian American Pacific Partnership (RAPP); Yuzhno-Sakhalinsk, Russia, July 14-17, 2003.

companies have expertise in offshore oil development, which is lacking in Russia, they are in an excellent position to participate in these projects.[229]

In recent years, Putin and Bush have stressed the general need to strengthen the relationship between the United States and Russia through greater commercial cooperation in the energy sector. Against this background and through a private-sector initiative, the Commercial Energy Dialogue (CED) was announced in October 2002 at the U.S.-Russia Commerical Energy Summit. It provides a forum for Russian and U.S. companies to discuss the most critical issues affecting the U.S.-Russia commercial energy relationship. The U.S. and Russian governments, at the same time, maintain regular consultations regarding the policy priorities emanating from these meetings and strive to implement the CED's recommendations.[230] Only the scope of future mutual achievements in the energy sector will show how effective these top-level business contacts between Americans and Russians actually are.

Institutional Partnerships

Many of the people-to-people contacts between Americans and Russians are taking place because both sides have established numerous institutional linkages from the mid- 1980s on. A White House release on American-Russian people-to-people cooperation from May 2002 reads,

> Currently, partnerships between American and Russian institutions are flourishing. They include 8 hospital partnerships, 37 university partnerships, and 94 Russian-American sister cities. More than 100 additional American-Russian community and institutional partnerships have also been forged between local governments, judges, businesses, professional associations, and other non-governmental organizations.[231]

The Russian-American Journalism Institute, for example, is a recent joint program of Rostov State University, New York University and Ithaca College, which brings together faculty and students from both countries. It is intended to strengthen the curricula and to improve understanding of international journalism at the schools.[232] In 2002, the William Davidson Institute (WDI) at

---

[229] Foundation for Russian-American Economic Cooperation (FRAEC); Internet site: <http://www.fraec. org> (accessed 18 October 2003). FRAEC is a non-profit organization founded in 1989 to foster expanded economic ties between Russia and the United States, and especially between the Russian Far East and the U.S. West Coast.

[230] American Chamber of Commerce in Russia (AMCHAM-Russia); Internet site: <http://www.amcham.ru> (accessed 14 October 2003).

[231] The White House Office of the Press Secretary, Fact Sheet: U.S.-Russian People to People Cooperation, May 24, 2002; Internet site: <http://www.whitehouse.gov/news/releases /2002/05/20020524-9.html> (accessed 25 October 2003).

[232] Russian-American Journalism Institute; Internet site: <http://www.itaca.edu/russia/ aboutenglish.htm> (accessed 8 October 2003).

the University of Michigan Business School (UMBS) and Urals State University (USU) in Ekaterinburg, have combined their efforts to establish the Russian-American Economic and Business Institute (RAMEC). Funded by federal grants, WDI and USU have held a number of institutional exchanges resulting in initiatives to assist USU in the creation of RAMEC. It is the first American-style applied economics education-research institution outside of the Russian capital. RAMEC is planning on welcoming students in September 2004.[233]

Under the auspices of Sister Cities International (SCI), with the assistance of USIA funding, more than 90 American cities have formed relationships with Russian sister cities.[234] David Potter, program officer for development at SCI, stated, "Nowhere ... has the impact of sister cities programs been more pronounced than between US cities and those of the former Soviet Union." The sister city programs are involving people at all levels. Professionals on both sides, as Potter demonstrates, view sister city affiliations as a means to establish business ties and to develop trade. One of the most exciting SCI programs links former "secret cities," scientific communities, which during the Cold War maintained laboratories and manufacturing facilities for nuclear weapons. Oak Ridge (Tennessee) and Obninsk have been sister cities since 1992. Los Alamos (New Mexico) and the Russian city of Saratov became partners in 1994. Livermore (California) and Snezhinsk have cooperated since 1996. In all three partnerships, over the years, nuclear scientists actively engaged in scientific exchanges and joint research projects.[235] In general, the sister city partnerships have formed the basis for many other projects, involving university programs, youth exchanges, and other people-to-people activities.

The mechanisms of community cooperation do not apply to cities only. The Buryat people of Lake Baikal in Siberia, for example, have formed a sister lake relationship with Lake Tahoe (California). In 1990, the Tahoe-Baikal-Institute (TBI) was established to help preserve both lakes. TBI is a non-profit organization registered in the United States and Russia with offices based in the cities of South Lake Tahoe (California), Incline Village (Nevada) and Irkutsk (Russia). The preservation is realized through research, environmental education programs, and international exchanges of scholars, students and practitioners in science, economics, policy, and other related disciplines. The creation of the Institute in both countries was unique among American-Russian partnerships when initiated. The idea and proposal for the joint initiative came from American and Soviet students at a 1988 international youth conference in

---

[233] Russian-American Economic and Business Institute (RAMEC); Internet site: <http://www.case.usu.ru/ en/about.php> (accessed 5 October 2003).
[234] All American-Russian sister city relationships are listed on the SCI Internet site: <http://www.sister-cities.org>.
[235] David Potter, „US-NIS Sister Cities: Building Community Partnerships That Last," Internet site: <http://www.isar.org/isar/archives/ST/sistercities471.html> (accessed 20 August 2003).

Helsinki, Finland, and was presented to Reagan and Gorbachev in person. As a result, a California Resources Agency delegation visited Lake Baikal in 1990 and negotiated an agreement with Siberian authorities calling for the creation of the Tahoe-Baikal Institute. Since its creation, according to TBI, over twenty international policy-maker and student exchanges have been hosted, and over forty projects in Russia, Mongolia, and the U.S. on environmental, economic and cultural issues have been developed. More than 200 international students have graduated from TBI's two-month summer exchange, where they discuss major environmental problems. They are guided on wilderness trips in the mountains surrounding both lakes and are involved in ecological fieldwork and research.[236]

Other institutional partnerships include school-to-school linkages, partnerships among museums, libraries or arts organizations. The High School Partnership Program, an initiative of President Reagan, established sister school partnerships to allowed high school students to visit and study in each other's countries for one month. In 1992 alone, approximately 1,100 students (500 Americans and 600 from the NIS) participated in this exchange program. With funds from the Freedom Support Act, USIA launched the Secondary School Initiative, which began in 1993. This exchange initiative has already brought together thousands of American and Russian students. In the early 1990s, an initiative called International Partnerships Among Museums, funded by USIA and administered by the American Association of Museums, supported exchanges of professional staff between the following: Chicago Historical Society with the Museum of Moscow Art Theater; Indianapolis Museum of Art with the Peter the Great Museum of Anthropology and Ethnography in St. Petersburg; Solomon R. Guggenheim Museum in New York with the State Russian Museum in St. Petersburg; and the Please Touch Museum of Philadelphia with the Museum of St. Petersburg.[237]

The Library of Congress and the Russian Book Chamber exchange tapes containing bibliographic data. With the Russian State Library, the Library of Congress concluded a general cooperation agreement in February 1997 that provides for joint efforts to align standards, to share electronic resources and to exchange bibliographic data. The New York Public Library exchanges materials and staff with St. Petersburg institutions, especially the Russian National Library.[238] A new and unusual joint library project is called *Meeting of*

---

[236] Tahoe-Baikal-Institute (TBI); Internet site: <http://www.tahoebaikal.org> (accessed 20 October 2003).
[237] USIA Fact sheet: „USIA Programs and Initiatives in NIS", Date: 19930402, PDQ database; Internet site: <http://pdq.state.gov>.
[238] Curt Weldon, US-Russia Partnership – A New Time, A New Beginning, pp 33-38, US-Russia Book Final, 11/6/01; Internet site: <www.house.gov/curtweldon/usrussia.pdf> (accessed 16 October 2003).

Frontiers. It is a digital library that chronicles the parallel experiences of Russia and the United States in exploring their frontiers and the meeting of those frontiers in the Pacific Northwest and Alaska. The Library of Congress concluded agreements with the Russian State Library (Moscow) and the National Library of Russia (St.Petersburg) regarding their participation in the project at the end of 1999. In the following years, the site was widely expanded. The *Meeting of Frontiers* website is intended for use in U.S. and Russian schools, libraries and by the general public in both countries.[239]

The ArtsLink Program, which is funded by a number of U.S. agencies, promotes international exchange and the building of partnerships between arts communities in Russia and the United States. It conducts professional exchanges for cultural professionals in the contemporary visual arts, performing arts and arts management.[240] In the American-Russian Youth Orchestra young Russian and American musicians are joined. The orchestra provides them with world-class training and touring opportunities in partnership with Russian and American cultural institutions. After Gorbachev came to power, *Project Harmony* was one of the first initiatives to promote cross-cultural contact between American and Russian youth. In Spring 1985, the first U.S. student choir group from Harwood Union High School in Vermont went to Leningrad, USSR. This first performing arts exchange led to more programs, supporting numerous youth performing arts exchanges between New England and people from all corners of the USSR. Today, *Project Harmony*, is involved in all kinds of exchange initiatives between Americans and Russians and administrates various projects in cooperation with Russian institutions.[241]

Americans in Russia

After the failure of détente, throughout the renewed cold war period of the early 1980s there were very few American tourists traveling to the USSR. However, when "Gorbymania" affected the American public in the mid-1980s, the number of American tourists to the Soviet Union started to increase, and at the end of the decade already exceeded 100,000 per annum.[242] After the USSR collapsed, as the graph in Fig. 7 shows, the rate of American travelers to Russia began to accelerate, and had tripled by 1995. Nonetheless, as the euphoria about the end of the Cold War ceased throughout the second half of the nineties, U.S. resident travel to Russia dropped in a parallel fashion. In 1999, the number of travelers

---

[239] Library of Congress, *Meeting Frontier*; Internet site: <http://www.frontiers.loc.gov/intldl/mtfhtml/mfhome.html> (accessed 11 November 2003).
[240] CEC ArtsLink; Internet site: <http://www.cecip.org> (accessed 23 October 2003).
[241] Project Harmony; Internet site: <http://www.projectharmony.org> (accessed 5 October 2003).
[242] Boyle, cited above, pp. 211, 238.

even fell below the level of 1990. In recent years, however, the number of Americans who traveled to Russia has grown again.

Fig. 7

U.S. Resident Travel to USSR/Russia
1990-2002

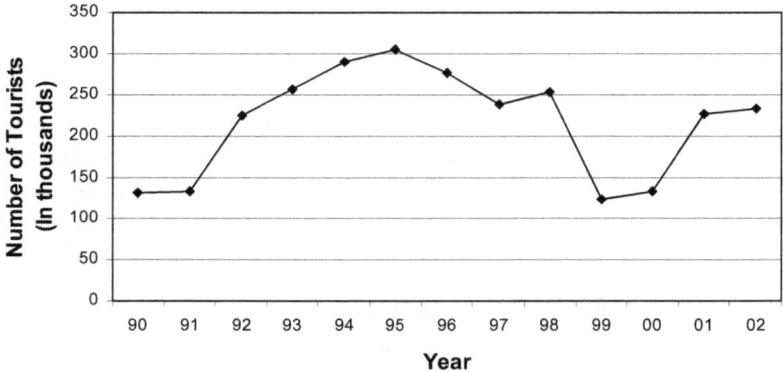

Source: U.S. Dept. of Commerce, International Trade Administration, Tourism, Industries; Internet site: <http://www.tinet.ita.doc.gov>

The real scope of U.S. resident travel to Russia only becomes clear when one compares it to the total number of Americans who travel abroad. At the peak in 1995, 0.6 percent of all Americans who traveled abroad, and 1.6 percent of those who traveled overseas visited Russia. Whereas the percentage of total U.S. resident travel abroad rose steadily throughout the late nineties, the percentage of those traveling to Russia decreased. In 1999, a mere 0.2 percent of all American international travelers, and a mere 0.5 percent of those who traveled overseas, went to Russia. In resent years, these percentages have increased again. Still, those Americans who travel to Russia today represent a very small part of total U.S. travel abroad. In 2002, for example, there were seven times as many Americans, who traveled to Germany.[243]

Although the 1990s witnessed an unprecedented number of Americans who experienced Russia for a longer period of time, either as professionals or as students, it was still insignificant in comparison to the number of Americans

---

[243] Source: U.S. Dept. of Commerce, International Trade Administration, Tourism Industries; Internet site: <http://www. tinet.ita.doc.gov> (accessed 19 December 2003).

who decided to work or to study in western European countries. For example, whereas in the academic year of 2001/02 more than 5,000 American students lived in Germany, the number of American students who spent an academic year in Russia never exceeded 1,200 throughout the last five years (see Fig. 8).

Fig. 8

American Students in Russia

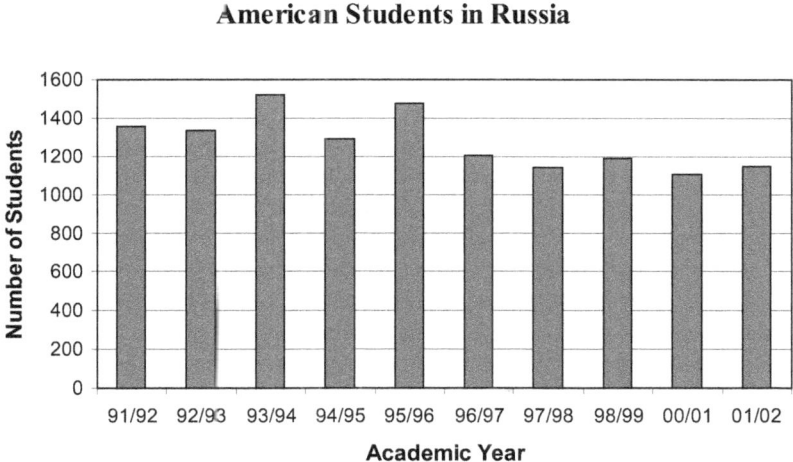

Source: Institute of International Education (IIE), Open Doors – Annual Reports on International Educational Exchange, Internet site: <http://opendoors.iienetwork.org>

Moreover, whereas the number of Russian students in the U.S. increased considerably throughout the 1990s (from approximately 1,600 in 1993/94 to more than 7,000 in 1999/00),[244] the number of American students who went to Russia did not change very much, and even decreased slightly throughout the second half of the 1990s.

---

[244] Source: Institute of International Education (IIE), Open Doors – Annual Reports on International Educational Exchange, Internet site: <http://opendoors.iienetwork.org> (accessed 12 October 2003).

14. Summary and Conclusions

Much of world history since the beginning of the 20th century, and particularly since the end of World War II, can be described in terms of Russian-American relations. Whereas the two world wars made Americans and Russians allies in the struggle against Germany, both nations opposed each other as the major warriors in the Cold War. In their fight against each other for global domination, the United States and the Soviet Union gathered allied states around themselves until the political world order had reached a state of bipolarity. For almost half a century, the main aim of American foreign policy was to maintain this balance of power. Americans feared, but at the same time were forced to respect, the Russians as the only other nuclear superpower in the world. Whereas the American image of Russia has changed several times throughout the first half of the 20th century (from a cruel autocracy, to an ally in World War I, then a cruel dictatorship, and again an ally in World War II), the image of a perceived enemy had not changed in the course of the following four decades. Under President Reagan, in the early eighties, the American public's fears and suspicions regarding the Soviet Union culminated for the last time within the Cold War era.

The coming of Gorbachev signaled the beginning of a revolutionary stage in American-Soviet relations. Gorbachev immediately took steps of rapprochement. This, along with his far-reaching reform ideas and his nice and pleasant personality caused widespread attraction to Gorbachev in the American media and public opinion, a mood, which was called "Gorbymania." The Soviet leader and the Soviet people came to be viewed increasingly in human terms. Negative perceptions of and feelings toward the USSR, which had continued for decades, had changed drastically in just a couple of years. From 1985 to 1990, the number of Americans who viewed the Soviet Union as a serious threat because of its military power, its struggle for world dominance or its generally perceived aggressiveness, decreased by half. Whereas in 1984 about 90 percent of Americans viewed the USSR either as an "enemy," or as "unfriendly," this percentage declined to a third by 1990. Accordingly, American hostility toward the Soviet Union declined sharply while at the same time the number of Americans who took a neutral or favorable stance increased considerably.

One of the main reasons for the declined perception of the Soviet Union as a threat was the signing of the INF treaty in 1987, which provided for the destruction of all intermediate-range nuclear weapons on both sides. The treaty had a particularly psychological effect on the American public since these weapons were considered most threatening because they were most useful for a preemptive attack. Due to the cautious reaction of the Presidents Reagan and Bush with regard to Gorbachev's wide-ranging offers, the amount of nuclear disarmament agreements in general was modest, and little progress was made in terms of economic relations. Nonetheless, during Reagan's second term as president the range of exchanges and interpersonal contacts between Americans and Russians swelled to an unprecedented flood. The occasions during which Americans met Russians ranged from government-to-government working groups and joint U.S.-Soviet space exploration projects, through so-called "citizen diplomacy" initiatives and youth exchanges. The number of American tourists in Russia had climbed to 100,000 per annum by 1990. Many of the currently existing American-Russian sister-city relationships had been established by the late 1980s.

Generally, from 1985 to 1990, Americans were increasingly eager to learn about the Soviet Union under Gorbachev. What happened in that country in these years, in the eyes of the majority of Americans, was of great importance to the U.S.' national interest. The events in the Soviet Union and Soviet-American relations received a record amount of attention in the American mass media. The number of evening news reports on the major TV news channels and the number of articles in the *New York Times* covering the Soviet Union exceeded even the amount of USSR coverage during the most intense periods of Cold War tensions. Student enrollments in Soviet area studies and Russian language study in the United States surged astonishingly during the excitement of the Gorbachev era, reaching a pinnacle around 1990.

Despite the omnipresent trend of optimism and hope, the American public was well aware of the fact that Gorbachev was a communist, and that he wanted to hold on to communism as the basis of the Soviet system. There was suspicion among many Americans that Gorbachev differed from previous Soviet leaders only in superficialities of style and appearance and that in fundamental objectives he did not differ at all from his predecessors. Decades of mistrust and the experience of failed détente in the 1970s, when Americans' hopes for a peaceful coexistence were dashed, made it this time much more difficult to overcome suspicions of the Soviets. The public mood in the late 1980s can be described as a cautious readiness; distinctly hopeful yet wary.

The Cold War was about ideology. The collapse of Soviet communist rule and the dissolution of the Soviet Union at the beginning of the 1990s marked the end of the Cold War. Now that ideology no longer divided the two countries, Americans' and Russians' interests seemed to be compatible. The most important interests of the United States were the maintenance of responsible control over the former Soviet Union's arsenal of weapons of mass destruction, Russia's integration into the world economy, its participation in a global security system that included the U.S. as well as Western Europe, its cooperation in resolving regional disputes, a working partnership in addressing global problems (such as international crime and terrorism) and its inner transformation into a market economy and stable democracy. Every one of these items was fully consistent with Russia's national interests.

The "honeymoon" period in American-Russian relations, although belated, saw the first important American assistance initiative for Russia and the other new countries of the former Soviet Union, the Freedom Support Program. It was meant primarily to support Russia in fostering the transition to a market economy and the democratization process. The American government fully endorsed a rapid economic reform, the so-called shock therapy, under Yeltsin. This tactic, however, was not reinforced socially or politically, and the painful consequences of the changes fell upon the Russian population. The Clinton Administration, captivated U.S. investors and many American academics and journalists enthusiastically embraced the idea of a virtual crusade to transform post-Communist Russia into a replica of America. They sought to teach Russians about economy and democracy, but Russia's reality proved them to be naïve and counterproductive illusionists. Russia experienced a massive human tragedy throughout the 1990s, with the worst economic depression in history, corruption, extensive capital flight, a crashed health care system, a demographic catastrophe and omnipresent poverty. Regardless, these virtual crusaders, and especially the American mass media, continued to portray Russia to be on its way to recovery. The bulk of American journalists, with regard to Russia's economic transformation, produced a false picture for the American public because they saw not what was, but what they wished to see.

In reality, the developments throughout the 1990s fell far short of the initially high expectations on both sides. Russia, at the end of the decade, had neither transformed into a flourishing market economy nor a stable democracy. The scope and anticipated effects of U.S.' financial assistance to Russia amounted to far less than what Russia had counted on. Russians' frustration over the role of the U.S. in the failing transformation was growing steadily. This, coupled with the perceived national humiliation due to Russia's downgraded role in world affairs and the American response to ignore Russia's interests (especially in terms of NATO enlargement to the east, and the appearance as "teachers" of Western virtues), culminated in an alarmingly wide-spread "new" anti-Americanism in Russia. These failures contributed heavily to the cooling period in the American-Russian relationship throughout the second half of the 1990s.

The frictions did not remain unnoticed by the American public. Shortly after the "honeymoon" period ended, the public's general perception of Russia witnessed a seven-year long cooling trend. Whereas in 1993, 66 percent of the Americans had a favorable perception of Russia, this percentage decreased to a mere 31 percent by 2000. Moreover, the disappearance of the "enemy" that needed to be known caused a tremendous decline in the Americans' interest in post-Soviet Russia. Since the collapse of the Soviet Union, Russia coverage in the American media had decreased by more than two-thirds in just a couple of years. Russia moved to the periphery of American public attention. Today,

Russia is hardly mentioned in the media, and the average American reader or TV viewer is extremely ignorant about Russia. In addition, enrollments in post-Soviet area studies and Russian language study have declined sharply since 1990.

As obvious as the discrepancies and misunderstandings between the two nations had been throughout these years, the bilateral relations were very productive. Some 97 agreements had been signed on the diplomatic level in just four years (between 1992 and 1996). They covered numerous aspects of cooperation, such as trade, investment, science, culture, humanities, education, and the mass media. On the people-to-people level these agreements led to widely enhanced American-Russian contacts. Increasingly, people on both sides were involved in mutual diplomatic and business-related activities, professional and educational exchanges and community and institutional partnerships. The first five years of the 1990s witnessed an increase in the number of American tourists, students, and business people heading for Russia. American travel to, and study in, Russia declined again in the course of the following five years. All in all, in the last two decades, Americans and Russians have developed sufficient mutual bonds which they can use as a solid basis for future cooperative activities.

Since Putin became president of the Russian Federation, the American relationship to Russia has been marked by ambivalent views and by ups and downs in terms of diplomatic cooperation. On the one hand, the mystery that surrounds the former KGB agent as a private person as well as a political leader caused uncertainties with regard to his commitment to democracy. On the other hand, Putin's ambitious legal and economic reforms, combined with his generally serious appearance, raised new hopes for an improvement of the petered out American-Russian relationship. The terrorist attacks of September 11, 2001, opened a new chapter in America's relationship with Russia. Americans and Russians, it became obvious, have a common enemy. While the Russian government and the Russian people expressed their sympathy with Americans in their hour of need and pledged support in the fight against terrorism, the United States curtailed its criticism of the Russian intervention in Chechnya. Both sides agreed on a New U.S.-Russian Relationship based on the mutual commitment to build a solid strategic partnership in order to cope with the new security threat. Russia's cooperation in the war on terrorism has further consolidated a recent warming trend in attitudes toward Russia among the American public.

Although other far-reaching steps of approach had followed, including the establishment of the NATO-Russia council, the conflict over the United States invasion of Iraq, in mid-2003, seemed to conclude an entire epoch in American-Russian relations. Russia's veto in the United Nations Council destroyed the American image of Russia as a serious and useful strategic partner. On the presidential level, however, both sides soon acted as if the recent conflict over Iraq had not hurt the fundamental partnership. Shortly after U.S. troops marched into Iraq, President Bush met Putin to congratulate him on the anniversary of St.Petersburg. Interestingly, the recent trend of warming American attitudes toward Russia did not alter because of the sparring over Iraq. Today, a majority of 58 percent of Americans have a favorable perception of Russia, viewing it either as "friendly but not a close ally" (43%) or even as a "close ally" (15%). A third of Americans have a neutral perception of their former enemy ("not friendly, not enemy") and only 10 percent still hold the view that Russia is "unfriendly and an enemy." It appears, that the Americans' relationship to and perception of Russia is strong and stable enough to overcome inconsistencies of great significance.

There is more than just one reason for this apparent stability in the American relationship to Russia. First, the general American view is that the interests both countries share greatly outweigh the interests that divide them. Russia's cooperation in the fight against terrorism and international crime, and its perceived potential of becoming an important economic power and trading partner in the future (due to the constant economic growth there in the last couple of years) are just two major factors that make it worthwhile for Americans to strive for a good relationship with the Russians. As most recent polls have shown, large majorities of Americans think of Russia as "vitally important" to U.S. interests, the fifth influential power in the world and a country that will play a greater role in the next ten years. Americans, although mostly ignorant about and uninterested in Russia, seem to be aware that it matters for three reasons: the atom (Russia is still a nuclear power.), the veto (in the United Nations Security Council) and the location (its proximity to the sources of potential threat to the U.S. and its huge energy resources). Less than two decades after the end of the Cold War, an astonishingly large majority of Americans wish to see Russia join NATO, a military alliance that was established with the specific purpose to fight the USSR in the case of war.

Notwithstanding these far-reaching steps of approach between Americans and Russians since the mid-1980s, the relationship between both countries is still on shaky ground. The "Great Transition," as the historian Raymond L. Garthoff called American-Soviet relations from the appearance of Gorbachev to the dissolution of the Soviet Union, is not yet over. Today, from a realistic American point of view, Russia is neither a foe nor a friend. Although the majority of Americans no longer perceive Russia as a national enemy or a threat to the U.S., they are still suspicious about it remaining a stable partner in the future. Whereas Americans and Russians have established many interpersonal linkages and have cooperated on a large scale in areas where they once opposed each other as competitors and arch rivals, the last decade has witnessed an alarming ignorance and lack of interest regarding Russia on the American side, and a so-called "new" anti-Americanism on the Russian side.

Russia no longer opposes the United States militarily. Although it works with the U.S. in regional conflict reduction (as in Bosnia and Kosovo), cooperates in the NATO-Russia Council and supports the U.S. in the fight against terrorism, it is still not a serious ally. While Russia has established a market economy, so far, it has still to cope with corruption, oligarchic structures and a generally low standard of living. It is still not a country the U.S. has reasonable trade relations with nor is it a country where Americans are eager to invest. Russia is still far from being a stable democracy. Although Russians generally favor democratic values, they differ on American principal believes in the sense that they are not fundamentally procapitalist, or anticommunist.

The Iraq experience demonstrates that the United States must change the format and the style of communications with Russia. To stabilize the relations with Russia, the United States must study its vital interests and establish a policy accordingly. In order to achieve the best possible basis for fruitful cross-cultural communication, Americans have to dismantle their stereotypes and instead familiarize themselves with the real differences between their own, and the Russian culture. Americans have been bridled with the task to overcome unrealistic expectations regarding a civilization, which in many aspects is so different from their own. In these turbulent post Cold War times, America is presented with the challenge and the chance to build a stable and lasting relationship with Russia. With Americans standing at a crossroads, understanding the Russians has never been so important since the end of the Cold War.

References

Abelman, Joan M.: Challenges to U.S.-Russian Cooperation in the Manned Space Program – A Research Report, Alabama, Air War College Air University, 1996.

Allison, Graham T.: Testing Gorbachev, in: *Foreign Affairs* 67/1, 1988, pp. 18-32.

Allison, Graham T., Robert Blackwill: America's Stake in the Soviet Future, in: *Foreign Affairs* 70/3, 1991, pp. 77-97.

Bardes, Barbara A., Oldenwick, Robert W.: *Public Opinion – Measuring the American Mind*, Toronto, Thomson & Wadsworth, 2003.

Bierling, Stephan G.: *Wirtschaftshilfe für Moskau: Motive und Strategien der Bundesrepublik Deutschland und der USA 1990-1996* (Economic Assistance for Moscow: Motives and Strategies of Germany and the U.S., 1990-1996), Paderborn, Ferdinand Schöningh,1998.

Black, Cyril E., John M. Thomson (eds.): *American Teaching About Russia,* Bloomington, 1959.

Bonnell, Victoria, George Breslauer: Soviet and Post-Soviet Area Studies, Berkley Program in Soviet and Post-Soviet Studies Working Paper Series, Berkley, University of California, 1998.

Boyle, Peter G.: *American-Soviet Relations – From the Russian Revolution to the fall of Communism*, London, New York, Routledge, 1993.

Brod, Richard, Elizabeth B. Welles: Foreign Language Enrollments in United States Institutions of Higher Education, Fall 1998, in: *ADFL Bulletin* 31/2, 2000, pp. 22-29.

Bronfenbrenner, Urie: The mirror image in Soviet-American relations, in: *Journal of Social Issues*, 17/3, 1961, pp. 45-56.

Brzesinski, Zbigniew: The Premature Partnership, in: *Foreign Affairs* 73/2, 1994, pp. 67-82.

Burn, Shawn M., Stuart Oskamp: Ingroup Biases and the U.S.-Soviet Conflict, in: *Journal of Social Issues* 45/2, 1989, pp. 73-89.

Cohen, Stephen F.: American Journalism and Russia's Tragedy, in: *The Nation*, Oct. 2, 2000.

Colton, Timothy J., Michael McFaul: America's real Russian Allies, in: *Foreign Affairs* 80/6, 2001, 46-58.

Cooper, William H.: Permanent Normal Trade Relations (PNTR) Status for Russia and U.S.-Russian Economic Ties, CRS Report for Congress, Order Code: RS21123, January 28, 2002.

Corley, William: Milestones in U.S.-Russian History – Market Economy Status, and a Little Respect, for Russia, in: *Export America*, July 2002, pp. 10-11.

Cortright, David: *Peace Works – The Citizen's Role in Ending the Cold War*, Boulder, San Francisco, Oxford, Westview Press, 1993.

English, Robert D., Jonathan J. Halperin: *The Other Side – How Soviets and Americans Perceive Each Other*, New Brunswick (U.S.A.), Oxford (U.K.), Transaction Books, 1987.

Erasov, B.S.: *Sotsial'naia kul'torologija*, Moscow, Aspect Press, 1997.

Garthoff, Raymond L.: *The Great Transition: American-Soviet relations and the end of the Cold War*, Washington, D.C., The Brookings Institution, 1994.

Garthoff, Raymond L.: The United States and the New Russia: The First Five Years, in: *Current History* 96/612, 1997, pp. 305-312.

Goldman, Stuart D.: Russia, CRS Report for Congress, Order Code IB92089, June 15, 2000.

Hoffmann, Stanley: The United States and the Soviet Union, in: Western *Approaches to the Soviet Union*, Michael Mandelbaum (ed.), Council on Foreign Relations Books, New York 1988, pp. 79-111.

Hogan, Michael J., Ted J. Smith: Polling on Issues – Public Opinion and the Nuclear Freeze, in: *Public Opinion Quarterly* 55, 1991, pp. 534-569.

Holt Robert R: College Students' Definitions and Images of Enemies, in: *Journal of Social Issues*, Vol. 452, 1989, pp. 33-50.

Legvold, Robert: Russia's Unformed Foreign Policy, in: *Foreign Affairs* 80/5, 2001, pp. 62-75.

Leontovitsh, O.A.: *Russkie i Amerikantsy: Paradoksy Mezhkul'turnovo Obshtshenia* (Russians and Americans: Paradoxes of Cross-Cultural Conversation), Volgograd, Peremena 2002.

Lipman, Masha: "Russia's Politics of Anti-Americanism," *Washington Post*, April 6, 2003; p. B07.

Luers, William H.: U.S. Policy and Gorbachev's Russia, in: *Gorbachev's Russia and American Foreign Policy*, Seweryn Bialer and Michael Mandelbaum (eds.), Boulder, London, Westview Press, 1988, pp. 409-435.

Mandelbaum, Michael: Ending the Cold War, in: *Foreign Affairs* 68/2, 1989, pp. 16-36.

Mommsen, Margareta: Das „System Jelzin" – Struktur und Funktionsweise des russischen „Superpräsidentialismus", in: *Demokratie in Ost und West*. Festschrift für Klaus von Beyme, Wolfgang Merkel, Andreas Busch (eds.), Franfurt a.M., 1999.

Nye, Joseph S. Jr.: Gorbachev's Russia and U.S. Options, in: *Gorbachev's Russia and American Foreign Policy*, Seweryn Bialer and Michael Mandelbaum (eds.), Boulder, London, Westview Press, 1988, pp. 385-408.

O'Connell, Social Charles Thomas: *Structure and Sciences: Soviet Studies at Harvard*, Doctoral Dissertation, UCLA, Department of Sociology, 1990.

Parks, J.D.: *Culture, Conflict and Coexistence – American-Soviet Cultural Relations, 1917-1958*, Jefferson (U.S.), London (U.K.), McFarland, 1983.

Paterson, Thomas G., J. Garry Clifford, Hagan, Kenneth J.: *American Foreign Relations, Volume 2 – A History Since 1895*, , Boston, New York, Houston Mifflin Company, 2000.

Raleigh, Donald J.: Doing Soviet History: The Impact of the Archival Revolution, in: *Russian Review* 61, 2002, pp. 16-24.

Richardson, Paul E.: The Decline of Russian, in: *Russian Life*, Jan/Feb 2001.

Richman, Alvin: The Polls – Poll Trends: Changing American Attitudes Toward the Soviet Union, in: *Public Opinion Quarterly* 55, 1991, pp. 135-148.

Richmond, Yale: *From Nyet to Da – Understanding the Russians*, Yarmouth, Intercultural Press, 1996.

Rosenthal, Andrew: "$ 1 Billion Credit to Soviets Urged," *New York Times*, October 23, 1991, A6.

Shearer, Ellen, Frank Starr: Through a Prism Darkly, in: *American Journalism Review*, Sept. 1996.

Shiraev, Eric, Vladislav Zubok: *Anti-Americanism in Russia*, New York, Palgrave, 2000.

Shuman, Howard, Ludwig, Jacob, Krosnick, John A.: The Perceived Threat of Nuclear War, Salience and Open Questions, in: *Public Opinion Quarterly* 50, 1986, pp. 519-536.

Sigov, Yuri: "Putin faces old struggle with U.S. media – Decades of negative mutual news coverage won't change overnight," in: *The Russia Journal*, November 16-22, 2001.

Silverstein, Brett, Catherine Flamenbaum: Biases in the Perception and Cognition of the Actions of Enemies, in: *Journal of Social Issues* 45/ 2, 1989, pp. 51-72.

Sloan, Stanley R., Steve Woehrel: NATO Enlargement and Russia: From Cold War to Cold Peace?, CRS Report 95-594 S. May 15, 1995.

Smith, Tom W.: The polls: American attitudes toward the Soviet Union and communism. in: *Public Opinion Quarterly* 47, 1983, 277-292.

Smith, Tom W.: The Polls – A Report: Nuclear Anxiety, in: *Public Opinion Quarterly* 52, 1988, pp. 557-575.

Solomon, Susan (ed.): *Beyond Sovietology: Essays in Politics and History*, New York, Armonk, 1993.

Stimson, James A.: *Public Opinion in America*, Boulder, Westview Press, 1999.

Tamoff, Curt: U.S. Assistance to the Former Soviet Union 1991-2001: A History of Administration and Congressional Action, CRS Report for Congress, Order Code RL30148, updated January 15, 2002.

White, Ralph K.: *Fearful Warriors – A Psychological Profile of U.S.-Soviet Relations*, New York, London, The Free Press, 1984.

Wolosky, Lee S.: Putin's Plutocrat Problem, in: *Foreign Affairs* 79/2, 2000, pp. 18-31.

Yankelovich, Daniel, John Doble: The Public Mood: Nuclear Weapons and the U.S.S.R., in: *Foreign Affairs* 63/1, 1984, pp. 33-46.

Yankelovich, Daniel, Richard Smoke: America's „New Thinking", in: *Foreign Affairs* 67/1, 1988, pp. 1-17.

Yatani, Choichiro, Dana Bramel: Trends and Patterns in American's Attitudes Toward the Soviet Union, in: *Journal of Social Issues* 45/2, 1989, pp. 13-31.

Internet Sources

U.S. Government Sources

Federation of American Scientists (FAS): http://www.fas.org

Meeting Frontier (LOC): http://www.frontiers.loc.gov/intldl/mtfhtml/mfhome. html

National Aeronautics and Space Administration (NASA): http://spaceflight.nasa. gov/home/index.html

National Security Education Program: http://nsep.aed.org

Open World Leadership Center: http://www.rlp.gov

Open World Program: http://www.openworld.gov

Public Diplomacy Query: http://pdq.state.gov

Ronald Reagan Presidential Library: http://www.reagan.utexas.edu

The White House: http://www.whitehouse.gov

U.S. Embassy to Moscow: http://www.usembassy.ru

USDA Forest Service: http://www.fs.fed.us/global/globe/europe/russia.htm

U.S. Department of Commerce, ITA: http://www. tinet.ita.doc.gov

U.S. Department of State: http://usinfo.state.gov

Polls and Statistics

Americans and the World: http://www.americans-world.org

Center for College and Pre-College Russian Language Studies (CCPCR): http://www.american.edu/research/CCPCR/infoorg.htm

Institute for Research in Social Science (IRSS), University of Noth Carolinahttp: http://www.irss.unc.edu/data_archive/ pollsearch.html

Institute of International Education (IIE), Open Doors – Annual Reports on International Educational Exchange: http://opendoors.iienetwork.org

Worldviews, a joint Chicago Council on Foreign Relations (CCFR) and German Marshall Fund of the United States (GMF) project): http://www.worldviews.org

NGO's and other Organizations

Alliance for American and Russian Women (AARW): http://www.aarwomen.org

American Chamber of Commerce in Russia (AMCHAM): http://www.amcham.ru

American Russian Center (ARC): http://www.arc.uaa.alaska.edu/index.htm

American Russian Law Institute (ARLI): http://russianlaw.org

Carnegie Endowment for International Peace: http://www.carnegie.ru

Center for Citzens Initiatives: http://www.ccisf.org

Citizen Exchange Council (CEC ArtsLink): http://www.cecip.org

CONNECT US/Russia: http://www.connectusrussia

Earth Island Institute: http://www.earthisland.org

Electronic Research Collection (ERC), a partnership between the United States Department of State and the Federal Depository Library at the Richard J. Daley Library, University of Illinois at Chicago (UIC): http://dosfan.lib.uic.edu

Foundation for Russian-American Economic Coop. (FRAEC): http://www.fraec.org

Initiative for Social Action and Renewal in Eurasia (ISAR): http://www.isar.org

Internews Russia: http://www.internews.ru

Project Harmony: http://www.projectharmony.org

Russian-American Economic and Business Institute, (RAMEC): http://www.case.usu.ru/en/about.php

Russian-American Journalism Institute: http://www.itaca.edu/russia/about english.htm

Sister Cities International: http://www.sister-cities.org

Tahoe-Baikal-Institute (TBI): http://www.tahoebaikal.org

The Nixon Center: http://www.nixoncenter.org

Appendix

Fig. 1

ATS: Americans Talk Security
CBS/NYT: Columbia Broadcasting System / *New York Times*
CCFR: Chicago Council on Foreign Relations
Gallup: Gallup Organization
Harris: Louis Harris and Associates
NORC/GSS: National Opinion Research Center (University of Chicago),
General Social Survey
PIPA: Program on International Policy Attitudes
Roper: Roper Organization
Time/CNN: Time/C News Network
Yankelovich: Daniel Yankelovich Group

Table 1

CBS/NYT: Right now, would you say the United States is superior in military strength to the Soviet Union, or is about equal in strength, or is not as strong as the Soviet Union?

Year	U.S. Not as Strong	About Equal	U.S. Superior	Don't Know
6/81	42%	39%	11%	8%
1/82	44	37	9	9
4/83	42	36	12	10
1/85	29	46	17	8
9/87	31	44	14	11
5/88	29	45	14	12
5/89	28	50	17	5
5/90	26	44	21	9

Table 2

Harris: Do you feel that Russia is a close ally of the U.S., is friendly but not a close ally, is not friendly but not an enemy, or is unfriendly and is an enemy of the U.S.

Year	Close Ally	Friendly, not close ally	Not friendly, not enemy	Unfriendly and enemy	D/K Refused
May 2002 ABC	10	53	24	7	7
Oct 2001 Harris	17	41	27	6	9
Aug. 2000 Harris	5	31	36	14	13
Sep. 1998 Harris	6	39	35	13	6
Sep. 1997 Harris	6	43	32	13	6
Nov. 1996 Harris	8	36	31	12	12
Oct. 1995 Harris	4	42	37	14	3
Mar. 1994 Harris	7	49	29	9	6
Apr. 1993 Harris	10	56	20	7	6

Table 3

Harris: Do you feel that Russia is a close ally of the U.S., is friendly but not a close ally, is not friendly but not an enemy, or is unfriendly and is an enemy of the U.S.

Year	Close Ally	Friendly, not close ally	Not friendly, not enemy	Unfriendly and enemy
Aug. 2003 Harris	15	43	32	10
Aug. 2002 Harris	14	44	34	8

Table 4

year	number of evening news	„Chechnya"/ „Iraq" – 2003
1968	529	
1969	725	
1970	529	
1971	826	
1972	368	
1973	277	
1974	445	
1975	533	
1976	590	
1977	896	
1978	1020	
1979	847	
1980	1263	
1981	1279	
1982	960	
1983	1207	
1984	1216	
1985	1247	
1986	1305	
1987	1290	
1988	1253	
1989	1296	
1990	1352	
1991	1158	
1992	474	
1993	390	
1994	385	57 (= 15 %)
1995	443	166 (= 38%)
1996	675	184 (= 27%)
1997	379	17 (= 3%)
1998	421	1
1999	500	155 (= 31%)
2000	438	124 (= 28%)
2001	192	10 (= 5%)
2002	161	49 (= 30%)
2003	166	Iraq : 79 (= 48%)

Table 5

Coverage of USSR/Russia-related topics in the *New York Times*

year	# articles	Foreign Desk	%	National Desk	%	Business Desk	%	Cultural Desk	%	"chechen /ya"	%	"crime"/ "criminal"	%	"corrupt (ion)" 12	%
80	527	339	64,3	39	7,4	44	8,3	16	3,0			22	4,2		2,3
81	941	535	56,9	80	8,5	120	12,8	14	1,5			54	5,7	10	1,1
82	871	544	62,5	60	6,9	92	10,6	18	2,1			40	4,6	20	2,3
83	1014	680	67,1	54	5,3	75	7,4	20	2,0			59	5,8	15	1,5
84	885	550	62,1	73	8,3	45	5,1	32	3,6			62	7,0	15	1,7
85	877	548	62,5	97	11,1	46	5,2	32	3,6			63	7,2	14	1,6
86	1011	639	63,2	99	9,8	42	4,2	41	4,1			55	5,4	26	2,6
87	1052	626	59,5	79	7,5	68	6,5	66	6,3			82	7,8	19	1,8
88	1116	575	51,8	80	7,2	105	9,4	91	8,2			76	6,8	33	3,0
89	1069	609	57,0	57	5,3	107	10,0	83	7,8			83	7,8	46	4,3
90	1052	604	57,4	35	3,3	173	16,4	54	5,1			74	7,0	35	3,3
91	1402	937	66,8	28	2,0	137	9,8	27	2,9	7	0,5	107	7,6	38	2,7
92	765	421	55,0	19	2,5	89	11,6	27	3,5	13	1,7	44	5,8	23	3,0
93	652	354	54,3	14	2,2	85	13,0	19	2,9	14	2,2	81	12,4	45	6,9
94	569	302	53,1	13	3,2	73	12,8	27	4,8	39	6,6	79	13,9	39	6,9
95	535	303	56,5	22	4,1	42	7,8	26	4,6	169	31,5	91	17,0	50	9,3
96	497	286	57,5	21	4,2	39	7,8	21	4,2	137	27,6	63	12,7	48	9,7
97	434	198	45,6	32	7,4	39	9,0	21	4,8	31	7,1	67	15,4	26	6,0
98	561	266	47,4	13	2,3	53	9,4	21	3,7	21	3,7	56	10,0	43	7,7
99	643	368	57,2	11	1,7	52	9,6	24	3,7	152	23,6	128	19,9	86	13,4
00	480	267	55,6	6	1,3	54	13,3	14	2,9	146	30,4	86	17,9	44	9,2
01	511	276	54,0	13	2,5	52	18,0	15	2,9	76	14,9	77	15,1	23	4,5
02	615	371	60,3	4	0,7	104	17,0	20	3,3	135	22,0	104	16,9	32	5,2
03*	474	270	57,0	9	1,9	87	18,4	20	4,2	82	17,3	110	23,2	40	8,4

* The figures for 2003 do not include the last two weeks of the year (December 20-31).

Table 6

	1986	1980	1986	1990	1995	1998
Spanish	32.4	41.0	41.0	45.1	53.2	55.0
French	34.4	26.9	27.4	23.0	18.0	16.7
German	19.2	13.7	12.1	11.3	8.5	7.5
Italian	2.7	3.8	4.1	4.2	3.8	4.1
Japanese	0.4	1.2	2.3	3.9	3.9	3.6
Chinese	0.4	1.2	1.7	1.6	2.3	2.4
Latin	3.1	2.7	2.5	2.4	2.3	2.2
Russian	**3.6 (4.)**	**2.6 (6.)**	**3.4 (5.)**	**3.8 (6.)**	**2.2 (8.)**	**2.0 (8.)**
Ancient Greek	1.7	2.4	1.8	1.4	1.4	1.4
Hebrew	0.9	2.1	1.6	1.1	1.2	1.3
American Sign Language	/	/	/	0.1	0.1	1.0
Portuguese	0.4	0.5	0.5	0.5	0.6	0.6
Arabic	0.1	0.4	0.3	0.3	0.4	0.5
Korean	0.01	0.04	0.1	0.2	0.3	0.4
Other Languages	0.7	1.4	1.3	1.2	1.5	1.5
Total	100.0	100.0	100.0	100.0	100.0	100.0
Total registrations	1,127,363	924,837	1,003,234	1,184,100	1,138,772	1,193,830

112

www.ingramcontent.com/pod-product-compliance
Lightning Source LLC
Chambersburg PA
CBHW022327280326
41932CB00010B/1260